THE OTHER SIDE
OF THE RAINBOW

with

Judy Garland
on the Dawn Patrol

THE OTHER SIDE
OF THE RAINBOW

with
Judy Garland
on the Dawn Patrol

---

by
MEL TORMÉ

WILLIAM MORROW AND COMPANY, INC.
New York 1970

FOR MY WIFE JAN

June, 1969

It was the largest turnout Campbell's Funeral Parlor had seen since that now-famous day back in the twenties when thousands of people had lined up to pay their last respects to Valentino, dead at thirty-one of peritonitis. Now, once again, thousands jammed the street. There were no hysterically shrieking women, but many people in the long queue wept unashamedly as they filed past the girl-woman lying in state inside Campbell's. On leaving the parlor, one middle-aged lady dabbed at tear-streaked cheeks with a piece of Kleenex and intoned, "Well, she's found that rainbow now."

"She," of course, was Judy Garland, dead at forty-seven. Her heart had stopped sometime during the early morning hours of June 22, probably owing to an accidental overdose of barbiturates. I say "probably," because most of her life had been so inexorably wound up in the use of sleeping pills coupled with periods of deep depression that no one may ever really know how or why she died. But she was gone now, and, ironically, the crowds in attendance during these last moments before the world lost sight of her mortal remains forever provided sharp contrast to the occasion of her recent marriage to Mickey Deans, thirty-five, a British discotheque manager. Everyone who was anyone in London was invited to the wedding reception. Nobody came. There were people there, to be sure. But the celebrities, Judy's "friends," stayed away in large groups. Someone at the reception was heard to remark, "Christ, even bloody Diana Dors didn't show up." Perhaps the Beautiful People of England's cinema colony were at last weary of yet another of Judy's peccadilloes. Perhaps they had heard her cry, "I have finally found true love," just once too often. Or perhaps every single one of them was engaged in pressing business affairs on that evening and just couldn't make it. One Hollywood producer smirked, "She's getting her comeuppance. Look how many times she didn't show up for a concert or a nightclub engagement. So now the tables are turned, and nobody shows for her wedding." Cruel, but possibly true. Judy's recent engagement at London's Talk of the Town was fraught with aborted performances, and it has been authoritatively reported that one particular audience threw food at her when she finally did appear, well over an hour late and allegedly under the influence. Very few sacred cows can and did get away with some of the things Judy did throughout her later life. But she prevailed. She created a mystique that served her well through some incredibly troubled times: broken marriages, suicide attempts, canceled appearances. The world seemed perfectly willing to give her one more chance in perpetuity. After all, she *was*

Dorothy. She had taken all of us to Oz, she had bravely defied the Wicked Witch of the West, once and forever shunting Margaret Hamilton into a niche in movie history, and she had sung "Over the Rainbow" so plaintively, with such bittersweet longing, that for every single patron sitting in a darkened theater, her pure, clear voice became a clarion call of half-remembered dreams.

And so they all came to Campbell's to say good-by. The curious, the sick-in-mind, the jaded few who viewed the whole thing as a "happening," the genuinely moved and saddened majority, silently remembering the Golden Days of Garland. And a few of her friends. Mickey Rooney, Ray Bolger. James Mason, who delivered the eulogy. And when Mason declared, "She was the most sympathetic, the funniest, the sharpest and the most stimulating woman I ever knew," he came as close to assessing her highly complex personality as one can get. Had he added the adjectives "frustrating, inspiring, devious, prank-loving, calculating," he would have also hit the marks. But he was delivering a eulogy, not a character analysis, and his remarks were as they should have been, proper and in good taste.

I did not know Judy Garland all her professional life. Born in Chicago, I lived there until I was sixteen, when I quit school temporarily to join the Chico Marx orchestra. I toured with the band for one year, during which time I was "discovered" by an RKO talent scout. When the band broke up in July of 1943, my mother, father, sister and I moved permanently to Los Angeles and I went into my first movie. It was during the making of this film that I met Judy for the first time. Or rather, saw her in person. I didn't meet her on that occasion; I will describe our meeting later on.

However, I was involved on an almost day-to-day basis

with her from May of 1963 until February of 1964, when I functioned as Special Musical Material writer and advisor on a CBS venture called "The Judy Garland Show" (or as one wag put it, "The Noble Experiment"). And that's what this book is all about.

THE OTHER SIDE
OF THE RAINBOW

with

Judy Garland
on the Dawn Patrol

Chapter 1

April 1963

The sound of the surf was soothing as it gently lapped against the shore. I took a sip of my drink, raised myself slightly from the deck chair and looked up. It was one of God's better days. Small fleecy clouds were scattered under an impossibly clear blue sky. The sun burned at just the right temperature; not hot enough to be uncomfortable, but perfect for getting a good even tan. Every fifteen minutes or so an old war-surplus Stearman buzzed the beach, dragging a sign advertising a restaurant or nightclub. Now, as the helmet-and-goggled pilot crabbed the biplane into the wind and headed up the coast, I casually looked around. The pool area was packed with laughing kids, gabby Jewish mothers, cigar-smoking, gin-playing men and some damned pretty girls in a variety of bathing suits. I leaned back into my deck chair, relishing the near-privacy of my cabana, and taking another sip of my drink, I sighed. After careful calculation, I decided I couldn't possibly stand more than fifteen or twenty weeks of this kind of life.

I was playing one of the leading hotels in Miami Beach and loving it. The band was good, the audiences warm and receptive, and, all things considered, I was relatively happy. I picked up my book and was about to begin reading when the poolside loudspeaker clicked on with a loud "pop" and a nasal Brooklyn accent blared forth: "Mr. Mel Tormé, lawng-distance telephone cawl." I laid the book down and picked up the cabana phone.

"Mr. Tormé?"

"Yes, operator."

"One moment, please." Pause. "Go ahead."

"Hello?"

"Hello, Mel?"

"Yeah, who's this?"

"Mel, this is George Schlatter."

"Hey, George, how are you?" (What the hell was George Schlatter calling *me* about, long distance yet. I barely knew him, having met him briefly when he had been a publicity man for Ciro's, Herman Hover's old, now-extinct Hollywood nightclub.)

We exchanged a few amenities, then he came to the point.

"Say, have you been reading the trades?"

"Uh . . . no, George, I haven't. I've been a little out of touch down here."

"I see. The reason I asked is, I'm involved in something really exciting for CBS. I'm going to be producing the new Judy Garland show and I've got a wild idea."

"Oh, really?"

"Yeah. I've decided the only guy in America good enough to write special music and lyrics for the show is you."

Schlatter is given to making broad, sweeping statements like that.

"Uh-huh. Well, George, that's very kind of you, but I don't really feel I'd be interest———"

"Think about it, Bunky. It's a great opportunity to do something really good on the tube. Sunday nights, nine o'clock, a great time slot. We're gonna knock *Bonanza* right out of the box."

"Well, George, I certainly wish you the best of luck and . . ."

"Like I said, think about it. I'll call you tomorrow." He hung up.

I went back to my chair, stretched out and thought about it. But not much. My immediate reaction was an obvious one; I felt insulted. Apparently George Schlatter thought my singing career was on the wane, that I wasn't "in demand" and that I could better use my time making other people look and sound good. In point of fact, I had to admit to myself, grudgingly, that he was partially correct. My career had reached a kind of plateau, and for the past year or two had remained as frozen as rent controls. But I had just done something constructive about the situation. I had shed a manager and taken on a new one, Joe Shribman.

Joe had always been one of my favorite people in the business. Big, warm, likable, scrupulously honest, he had served his apprenticeship within the boundaries of his own family, the famous Shribman clan that had guided the destinies of the Big Bands and made household names of Glenn Miller, Artie Shaw et al. Joe, for the past twelve years, had managed Rosemary Clooney. Now he had recently married Temple Texas, a former showgirl and publicity agent, and he wanted to "get off the road" and settle down in a house in Los Angeles. When he found, to his delight, that I was one of the few singers who did not want or need an entourage traipsing around the country with me, he agreed to become my manager. Our alliance spelled a new beginning for me. Already he had secured a multiple-guest-shot deal for me on the then-popular Garry Moore TV show. He was huddling with Columbia records, negotiating a new recording contract, and through the mystical force of his own devices, had booked several upcoming nightclub dates at a substantial increase in salary for me.

I picked up my book once more and promptly forgot the phone call.

The next day, however, was something else again. Schlatter called not once, but twice, extolling the virtues of "the project," regaling me with stories about "the new Garland," piquing my interest with a roster of the excellent crew he was gathering together to help Judy "knock *Bonanza* out of the box."

After he hung up for the second time, reminding me to "think it over, Bunky, we gotta have you," Shribman called me. Schlatter had also been on the phone to him several times, and he felt he should at least apprise me of this. I told Joe I was trying hard to feel insulted, but that George's persistence was certainly rather flattering. I also remarked that Schlatter was cornering the market on the finest talent in the television industry. He had already signed one of the best scenic designers, Gary Smith, as well as Bill Hobin, a highly respected director. I also told him that I just wasn't interested in Schlatter's proposition. Shrib didn't argue the point. He had been working hard, putting new life into my career, and I felt he shared my reluctance to suddenly subordinate my own singing status and chain myself to a piano for someone else. Joe and I said good-by on a note of mutual agreement, and I was happy to have made a joint decision with my new manager predicated on good, sensible thinking. That was the end of that, I thought. But I hadn't reckoned with George Schlatter's tenacity.

Later that day, the phone rang again.

"Mel, this is George again."

"Yes, I know. Hi, George."

"Listen, I talked to Shribman, and, uh, he said you said no. Definitely."

"That's right, George."

"I don't understand, Buddy. Why?"

What I had thought was a well-controlled albeit somewhat injured ego came rushing up from my groin, whistling through my lungs and spewing out of my mouth.

"Jesus, George, does it occur to you that I have a rather important singing career of my own to worry about?" I won't sicken you with what followed. Suffice it to say I ran the gamut of injured pride, informing him of my upcoming Garry Moore commitments, nightclub dates, recording contract.

I must say he took this tiny tirade affably. When it had run its course, he said, thoughtfully, "Look, Bunky, would you consider coming to work on the show if we guaranteed you, say, two guest shots in the first thirteen?" He paused to let this sink in. "I mean, you'd have the opportunity to sing with Judy, and you would write the duets yourself. You'd really have some creative control for a change."

I thought about it for a minute. "George, you're a hard guy to turn down," I said.

He laughed. "It's my boyish charm. Seriously, how about it?"

"I don't know. I just don't know. Are you sure you can deliver Judy every single week? From all I've heard and seen of her, she's not the most disciplined lady in show biz."

"Let me worry about that," he replied. "We're gonna make this so much fun for her, she'll show up an hour early every day."

I was silent for a moment. "O.K., let me think about it a little more this afternoon, I'll call you and give you my answer tonight."

He seemed relieved. "Great. I'll look forward to hearing from you. And Mel," he added, probably as a balm to my wounds, "it won't hurt your image one bit to write for Judy. For any other singer, maybe, but not for Judy. Remember, she's the last of the real superstars, now that Jolson's gone." He hung up, and I tried to find some comfort in his last remark.

That night, after my first show, I took a walk along the beach, trying to sort out my sudden ambivalence. I had said no, flatly. Now I was actually considering his proposal. On one hand I was still stubbornly sticking to my mental guns. This was no time in my life to virtually chuck the immediate prospects Joe had been working on and semi-bury myself in an office (already I was weakening, already I had mentally altered "bury" to "semi-bury"). On the other hand, however, here was a chance to revitalize my writing and composing, to flex dormant muscles. The Rock 'n' Roll era had sapped my initiative as a songwriter. Too many frightened publishers had listened to my tunes and remarked, almost sadly, "They're good, Mel. They're *too* good." When I had heard enough left-handed compliments of that kind, I had cleaned my old Esterbrook music-writing pen and laid it carefully away in a drawer. "The Judy Garland Show" could be a good reason to put that pen back into use (and my brain along with it). The idea of two guest shots in that time slot was also tempting. More important, I would be able to stay home for a while. I had a house in Beverly Hills, a three-year-old son and a doomed marriage that I thought might be worth saving. Overriding all the foregoing, were my doubts about Judy herself. Her lack of professional discipline and her erratic personal behavior were no secret to anyone who had the price of a newspaper. Ten years ago she had made *A Star Is Born;* the problems, delays and exorbitant costs encountered in the shooting of the film stood as sorry landmarks of disaster until *Cleopatra* and Brando's *Mutiny on the Bounty* finally wiped them from memory. Her recent concert dates were enormously successful, but on innumerable occasions she showed up late and in many instances not at all. Now, CBS was going to gamble on her well-known instability, and worse, throw her into the Sunday night nine o'clock arena, against the mammoth perennial *Bonanza.* It had all the aspects of legalized murder. And yet . . . if Schlatter *could* get her to show up, if he really could make it so exciting for her that her competitive juices would bubble over and stimulate her incentive, then, by God, she might just be the one person living who could indeed knock the lofty *Bonanza* "out of the box."

I looked at my watch. Plenty of time before the next show. It was a balmy evening, with a full moon flooding the night sky, making a thick, irregular path of light on the water. I sat down on the beach and thought about the first time I ever saw Judy Garland in the flesh.

1943

I had come to Los Angeles to live. The Chico Marx band was now history. But I had been seen by RKO talent scout Arthur Willy during my tenure with the band. We had been appearing at the Roxy Theater in New York City, and I had a featured spot in the show. Willy saw me and arranged for a silent test to be shot, on the roof of the Roxy, no less. He subsequently informed me that the test was successful and that RKO had signed me for the juvenile lead in a picture called *Higher and Higher,* to be shot in Hollywood in August or September of that year. The breaking up of the band in San Francisco in mid-July coincided perfectly with my starting date on the picture. The stars of the film were Michele Morgan, Jack Haley, Victor Borge, and, in his first starring role, Frank Sinatra. I played opposite a little redheaded pepperbox named Marcy McGuire.

One day, as we were breaking for lunch, Marcy asked me if I would like to escort her to a party that night. I nodded and said, "OK," but I was secretly thrilled. It would be my first Hollywood party, and for a kid from Chicago who ate, drank and slept movies and had been doing so since he was old enough to walk, this would be the penultimate experience.

I picked Marcy up in a little sand-colored Plymouth convertible, bought for me just a few weeks earlier by my doting Grandpa Sopkin, and we headed over Laurel Canyon out to the Valley. The party was being held (don't laugh!) in a large barn. The occasion was the eighteenth birthday of the current king of teen-age movie performers, Donald O'Connor. Everyone was dressed in farmer-type overalls, gingham dresses and straw sombreros. The place was jammed with the young Hollywood set, and with a band swinging the latest Tommy Dorsey hit and the dance floor a wriggling, writhing mass of jitterbugs, the whole scene looked like an "out-take" from one of Donald's pictures, complete with the "Jivin' Jack and Jills."

Marcy promptly went Hollywood on me and disappeared into the crowd, leaving me with a large quantity of egg on my face, alone and unknown, standing there like a real *klutz,* wanting badly to talk and be talked to. As I looked around I recognized many young actors and actresses I had admired and envied as a moviegoer back in Chicago. There, just a few feet away, was Dickie Moore. And over there, talking animatedly were Ann Gillis, Peggy Ryan, Marcia Mae Jones, Scotty Beckett, Cora Sue Collins. And there, sitting in a chair against the wall, alone and completely lost, was Judy Garland.

She was twenty-one at the time, and looked fifteen. She was wearing a white dirndl dress, her dark hair pulled back with a green ribbon, and her famous Keane-painting eyes were larger than I had remembered them in her movies. She seemed ill at ease, and somehow, vulnerable. Occasionally, someone would stop to say something to her, but the conversation was always brief, and once again she would be left alone, looking like nothing so much as the classic wallflower. Perhaps they were all in awe of her that night. Maybe they felt as if she were sitting there, holding court in some private way of her own and that the closest they ought to get to her was a brief word of hello, a respectful acknowledgment, a small moment of homage. Later in life, she always claimed the young Hollywood clan could never relate to her socially, that she was shunned and ignored at parties. That first time I saw her at the O'Connor party has always remained with me, and I think she was right.

At twenty-one, she was very much a woman physically, despite her deceptively youthful appearance. Her two-year-old marriage to composer David Rose was in disrepair. She had for some time relied on sleeping pills to help diffuse the insecurity that wracked her mind and body nightly, leaving her sleepless and unequipped to perform before the cameras on countless mornings. Yet, she had created the image of the typical American teen-ager so well that she was still regarded as a "kid" star in Hollywood and was automatically invited to most of the juvenile parties such as the O'Connor affair.

I wanted to walk over, introduce myself, engage her in conversation. But I didn't. I was determined not to be pushy, and I let the opportunity pass.

1949

The next time I saw her was on the MGM lot. I was under contract to the studio for three pictures. The second of these was in production. The film was based on the life stories of Rodgers and Hart and was called *Words and Music*. In a sequence that supposedly took place at Lorenz Hart's Hollywood mansion, I played a bandleader who sang "Blue Moon" at one point during an evening's festivities. I had already recorded and filmed my number, but because of my bandleading role, I was required to remain on hand for the filming of "Wish I Were in Love Again," a duet between Judy and Mickey Rooney, who played Hart in the picture. Mickey, the consummate pro, was there, bright and early in the morning, ready to work. Judy, on the other hand, was nowhere to be seen. The Mick and I had become friends in recent years, and I asked him whether he thought she would show up. Mickey had always maintained a cavalier attitude toward Judy. He looked me right in the eye and said: "Pal, if she isn't here, there's a damn good reason for it. And when she shows—and she'll show, believe me— she'll jump right in and be the best frigging thing in the picture!"

For two days, we waited—Mickey, and I, and director Norman Taurog and many dress extras—reading, playing cards, being entertained by the mighty Rooney, until at 3:00 P.M. on the third day, Judy arrived. She seemed nervous and tired, but she proceeded to "jump right in and be the best frigging thing in the picture." One night, not long after the completion of *Words and Music,* I had dinner at Mickey's house. When Judy's name was brought up, he smiled and reminded me of that day on the set. "Judy," he said, "has the uncanny ability to get in there and 'pull it off.' When we made *Babes in Arms* and *Strike Up the Band* she winged some of the numbers without a hell of a lot of rehearsal, and they worked out just great."

I had to agree, but I asked him if he didn't think the same numbers would have been even greater with a bit more preparation. Mickey shook his head and waved this aside. "You don't understand, kid. It's this spontaneous thing she has that makes her unique." When that evening was over, Mickey left no doubt in anyone's mind that he was Judy's mentor, fan and friend. As far as he was concerned, she could do no wrong, and though I went away feeling he was rather blindly biased where she was concerned, I had to admit it would be comforting to have a devoted champion like the Mick.

1951

At the Palace Theater, Judy made history. Tickets were impossible to get. The reviews were stunning. It was one of the greatest single comebacks in the annals of show business, rivaled only, perhaps, by the Al Jolson renaissance a few years earlier. I was living in New York, doing a daily daytime television show for CBS. The repeated question, "What? You haven't seen Judy at the Palace yet?" bounced in and around my ears like a swarm of hornets. I finally got tired of being admonished by one and all, and paid scalper's prices for a ticket to an evening performance.

My seat was far back enough and high enough to be in the direct flight path of incoming traffic at La Guardia, but it didn't matter. The moment Garland stepped onto the stage and proceeded to dazzle the packed house with "Swanee," "Rock-a-bye Your Baby," "San Francisco" and the myriad other Garland classics, I finally knew what everyone had been shouting about. And the final pin-dropping moments when she sat, in the tramp costume on the edge of the stage, legs dangling over, lighted only by a single spotlight, and sang "Over the Rainbow" was for me, and everyone else, one of the few really great pieces of theater we would ever see.

I went backstage after she had taken her twelfth or thirteenth curtain call. She was flushed with excitement, success. She hugged me, motioned to a chair. She had looked deceptively thin from my balcony seat. Now, up close, she seemed heavier, although not unattractively so. She grinned at me, offered me a drink, and said: "Well, Melvin?"

I raised my hands helplessly. "What can I possibly say that you haven't already heard?"

She smiled. "I don't know. Try."

"All right. It was one of the few emotional experiences I have ever had in a theater. It was . . . too much to digest at one sitting. I'm simply going to have to come back and see it again."

The smile remained, but she said, surprisingly, "No, don't."

"Don't? What do you mean?"

"Just that. Don't come back."

"Come on, you're kidding."

"No, seriously, you should only see me once. You'll be disappointed the second time."

"Judith, you're out of your gourd."

She grimaced knowingly. "You'll see," she said.

Two weeks later I returned to the Palace. The reception and attendant ovation for her was, if anything, greater than on the previous occasion. But I saw what she meant. I wasn't really disappointed, but having reacted to the first performance on a purely sensory basis, I was now inured enough to examine her act technically. When she sang "Over the Rainbow," the tears rolled down her cheeks at the precise moment they had flowed the last time I had seen her. Later, in her dressing room, she said, "You were surprised when I cried 'on cue' in 'Rainbow,' weren't you? Now admit it, bub, you were surprised and disappointed."

"Like hell I was," I countered. "It just reaffirmed what I already knew; you're not only one hell of a singer, you're a tremendous actress."

"I know," she nodded, without a drop of conceit, merely acknowledging a proven fact. "But sometimes when I turn the tears on, people who have seen me here before go away disappointed." She seemed happy to find I was not.

After the Palace, she repeated her triumph in London and on a long string of concert dates in America. Soon stories began to filter through. She was arriving twenty minutes to an hour and a half late for her concerts. She was drunk more than half the time. Promoters were forced to refund the customers' money in many instances. Judy was "up to her old tricks."

I was saddened to hear these stories. She had seemed so happy at the Palace, with her newly regained prominence. Apparently the complicated jigsaw puzzle that was Judy Garland seemed to be breaking apart. Perhaps the irregular pieces of her psyche could never be put back together again. I remembered Mickey's blind faith in her ability to "pull it off," to "bounce back," and I mentally wished her good luck.

1954

I was appearing at the Crescendo nightclub on Sunset Strip. One Thursday evening, just before my midnight performance, the maître d' informed me that Frank Sinatra had made a reservation for the show and was bringing in Judy Garland. I was delighted and nervous. Sinatra had been my favorite singer and influence since his early days with the Harry James band. I was still starry-eyed about Garland, and the thought of the two of them at the same table, watching a performance of mine, made my palms perspire.

They were seated ringside shortly after I began my opening song. Judy looked beautiful, bright-eyed, happy. I was determined to try and sing "over my head" that night.

While I have never been totally satisfied with *any* performance I have given, I walked off the stage feeling I had come close to being really good. While Sinatra appeared unimpressed, applauding only politely, Judy's obvious exuberance over my work more than made up for the disappointment I felt. She came down the stairs to the dressing room, hugged me and was warmly complimentary. She sat there with me, having a drink, telling a few stories, being totally charming and effusive, until word came down that Frank was in a bad mood and, in fact, had tangled physically with my press agent. Judy excused herself, kissed me on the cheek, praised my performance once more and walked out of the room, leaving me with a slightly swelled head and a warm glow around the cardiac region. I wanted, more than anything else, to call Mickey Rooney at that moment and agree with him unconditionally about his friend (and mine), Judy Garland.

Now, nine years later, Judy was embarking on a perilous journey into the jungles of television, and once again, she would need a large quantity of luck.

The moon was higher in the sky, and it was nearly time for my second show. As I walked back toward the hotel I thought hard about the pros and cons of writing the Garland show for CBS. She had had difficulty all her movie life adapting herself to the routine of toiling before the cameras. The responsibility of starring on a weekly hour-long television series might prove even more burdensome than the old MGM days. The "tube" was a terribly intimate medium. Flawed performances, unprepared sketches, lack of attention to detail, suffered with merciless clarity when viewed in one's home from a distance of a few feet.

Still, CBS must know what they're doing, I thought. And George Schlatter. *And* the talented people already signed for the show. Perhaps Judy realizes that finally, after being exploited and underpaid at MGM all those years, she is about to own a substantial piece of a property that could drive away insecurity forever. In fact, if she *did* buckle down and work her little *tush* off to make the TV show a huge hit, she would probably never have to work again for the rest of her life.

I entered the hotel and went up to my room to change. I stared at the telephone for a long time. I looked at the clock on the nightstand. It was 9:00 P.M. in Los Angeles. Impulsively I went to the phone, picked it up and gave the operator a number. When he answered the phone, I said, "George, this is Mel Tormé. OK. You've got me. Now where and when do you want me to go to work?"

Chapter 2

Since preproduction was to begin around the first of June, I quickly started to get some of my prior commitments out of the way. One of these took me to New York in mid-May for an appearance on the Garry Moore television show. No sooner had I settled into my hotel suite than I got a call from Schlatter.

"Hiya, Melvin."

"George? How's the weather out in Tinseltown?"

"I'm here, buddy. In New York. We're all here."

"Who is 'we'?"

"Oh, Johnny Bradford, the Waldmans, Judy———"

"Judy's *here* with you?"

"Yeah. Hey, man, she looks great! She's the old Judy again."

He went on to explain that they were all in town for a big CBS dinner, which was to take place that night at the Waldorf. All the affiliates, all the executives from every part of the country would be there. The highlight of the evening was going to be the surprise appearance of Judy. It would be her introduction to the network bigwigs and their wives. She was even going to sing for them. George could hardly contain his excitement.

"And wait till you hear *what* she's going to sing!"

"I'm all ears."

"Naw, naw, it's too beautiful to tell you on the phone. Come on over and say hello."

I took a cab over to the Waldorf and went up to Schlatter's suite. Johnny Bradford, who had been signed as head writer, greeted me at the door. We were old acquaintances. His brother Bob Wells and I had been song-writing partners years earlier. Together, we had turned out "The Christmas Song." Johnny was as unlike Bob as brothers could possibly be. Bob was a natural athlete, excelling in golf, skeet shooting or anything else he decided to tackle. Bradford, on the other hand, was slim—no, he was *thin*—graying, with a sallow complexion and a perpetual pair of dark half-moons under the eyes. He looked like most of the writers I knew who were constantly plying their trade indoors, and in a sudden burst of reverse Walter Mittyism, I pictured myself hunched over a piano in a dingy cubicle somewhere in the nether reaches of the vast CBS complex, a cheerless, airless musical prison cell wherein I would grind out reams of special material for Judy Garland. At that precise moment I was suddenly positive I was going to wind up as a sort of latter-day Uriah Heap, and I nearly bolted for the safety of the elevator. But Johnny's ebullience shook me out of my mini-reverie.

"Jesus, it's good to see you. Come on in. George is shaving; he'll be out in a minute. Hey, do you believe this whole thing? Isn't it wild?"

Since Johnny had always impressed me as being cool, contained and not given to enthusiastic outbursts, I was happy to see Schlatter's fine hand at work on someone other than myself. If *everyone* was this excited about the Garland show, it ought to be the winner of all time. We chatted for a few moments until George joined us.

George Schlatter had been a publicity man for a great deal of his professional life. When television became a practicality after the war, he saw the light and set himself the task of becoming a producer. The natural glibness, the ability to "talk on your feet" that is the stock-in-trade of every good PR man stood him in good stead. Of slightly more than medium height, his stockiness, dark brown hair, roundish face and mischievous smile made for a perennially boyish appearance. You just naturally wanted to do things for George; he was that likable. CBS certainly must have thought so. "The Judy Garland Show" was undeniably a plum. The trick was to keep from choking on the pit.

George wrung my hand, treated me to a dazzling smile. "Hey, tiger," he beamed, "we're gonna have the world by its thing. We've got the biggest star in the business, the best talent to make her look good, the whole *schmear*. Want a drink?"

"No thanks," I said. He poured himself one, smiled at me again and said, "Man, I can't wait to get started."

"Yeah," agreed Bradford, "it's gonna be a gas."

They both looked at me, waiting for a response. I grinned a bit self-consciously. "OK, OK. But listen, Orville—Wilbur: will it fly?"

Schlatter's smile turned Machiavellian. "It'll fly. You better believe it'll fly. It'll soar, baby. It's gonna be the god-dam mother show of all time."

"How . . ." I asked haltingly, not wanting to be a bucket of cold water in this steam room, "how does Judy feel about . . ." I searched for the right word ". . . everything?" I ended lamely.

George laughed happily. "How does she feel? How—does—she—FEEL?" He waved airily toward Johnny. "Sing it for him."

Johnny grinned broadly as Schlatter said, once again, "Go on, go on, sing it for him!"

"I wrote this parody for Judy. She's singing it tonight at the CBS dinner."

"She flipped when she heard it," added George. "She laughed her ass off."

"Now dig," said Johnny. He began to sing a parody to a well-known song of the day. It went, roughly, like this:

> Call me irresponsible
> Call me unreliable
> Throw in undependable too
> Do my foolish alibis bore you
> Are you worried I might not
> show up for you?

George chuckled. "How about that? They'll fall off their chairs tonight. 'Do my foolish alibis bore you?' " He laughed out loud. "Wow! Now that's funny! And guys;" he added, suddenly serious, "that's what this whole thing is all about. We've got to keep Judy light and funny. We've got to *humanize* her. Without, of course, damaging her image. That's her great value. She's really the last of the superstars. We've got to find a way to capitalize on that and at the same time make her come across warm and human on the tube.

When you're coming into their front rooms, nine o'clock Sunday nights, they've got to be able to identify with you. We've got to make Judy appeal to the whole family."

"Like *Bonanza*?" asked Bradford.

Schlatter frowned. "Go wash your mouth out with soap." He turned to me. "How about it, Bunky, you got the picture?"

I paused, thinking about it for a moment. I was still rolling the parody around in my head, wondering if it really *was* such a good idea. After all, it was to be Judy's first exposure to the CBS hierarchy, and what if . . . Oh, what the hell, I thought suddenly. Let it happen, don't be a gloom spreader, Tormé.

"Gee, I don't know about you guys," I smiled brightly. "I'm flying the mail to Pittsburgh!"

Since I was rehearsing the Moore show that evening, I wasn't able to attend the dinner. I wanted to say hello to Judy before I left, but George told me she was resting and that he would say hello for me and that I would see her on the Coast in a couple of weeks. I left the Waldorf with mixed emotions. I was eager to get to rehearsal, but I found myself regretting not being able to be with the Garland team that evening.

I returned to California a few days later. I was living in Beverly Hills in a large, neo-modern house. My wife had purchased it in a burst of status-building frenzy. Although the Garland show was not scheduled to commence for another week or so, I began putting some ideas together. It seemed a good way to get a head start on what I knew would shortly hit the fan.

The brain is a wholly predictable muscle. Like the biceps, triceps or pectorals, it begins to function dependably if you flex it and continue the exercise. Rock 'n' Roll was in its infancy. Its juvenilistic three-chord form was prevalent, and to turn on most L.A. radio stations was to invite inundation by unintelligible singers and groups. The refinement of the art as practiced by Lennon and McCartney, Simon and Garfunkle, and Burt Bacharach was a few years away. Most music publishers were running scared, and to bring them a sophisticated song was tantamount to self-induced masochism, in short, instant refusal. As a composer-lyricist, I found this state of affairs depressing. My natural initiative to write had been badly squelched for some time.

Now, suddenly, I was writing again and enjoying it. There was a kind of freedom in creating special material. I wasn't restricted by current pop musical tastes. By the time Schlatter called me and said, "Come on in, we're ready to roll!" I had a substantial amount of music and lyrics to submit.

The Garland offices were situated on the third floor of CBS Television City, at the corner of Fairfax and Beverly Boulevards. As I drove toward the Artists Entrance gate, I looked around and felt a small pang of nostalgia. Where TV City now stood, there had once existed Gilmore Stadium, the home of the Mighty Midgets. Auto racing during the years immediately after the war was practically the official city pastime, and Gilmore was considered the finest quarter-mile midget-auto racing track in the country. On Thursday evenings, I had religiously made my way through streams of traffic to watch my favorites—Duke Nalon, Bullet Joe Garson, Ed Haddad and Johnny Parsons—tool their gleaming little Offys around the oval. The smell of racing fuel in the air was an aphrodisiac. Now it was gone. In its place was the enormous black-and-white building CBS had built to house its television operation. It was beautiful and functional, but it wasn't Gilmore. I regarded it for a moment, thought back once again to those happy days in the stands with clods of dirt coming at you from the broadsiding racers. "Progress," I sighed, and drove on in.

I got off the elevator at the third floor, rounded a corner and headed in the direction to which the receptionist had pointed. I found a door that announced the room behind it as housing "The Judy Garland Show." As I reached for the knob, it was opened from the inside by George Schlatter. He greeted me with his usual effusiveness, then stepped into the hall, closely followed by Johnny Bradford, and Tom and Frank Waldman, who had been signed as writers. George introduced me to the Waldmans and, motioning us to follow him, started walking briskly down the hall.

"What's up?" I asked Johnny.

"We're on the way to look at the stage."

We went down to the first floor and stopped in front of Stage 43. George grinned happily and pointed to the bottom of the stage door. "How about that," he beamed. The art department had painted a winding yellow brick road from the entrance of the stage clear across the hall to the steps of a large yellow house trailer, situated in the corner of the first-floor hallway and looking ludicrously out of place. Little red footsteps had been painted on the bricks leading to the trailer, and I had to close my eyes and shake my head to keep from hearing Toto and the Cowardly Lion gamboling gaily in the men's room nearby.

"Judy's gonna love that," exulted George. "And her trailer." He opened the stage door, and we all followed him in.

Stage 43 was a big, deep studio, with the bulk of the depth allotted to the stage itself. It had been completely refurbished for Judy. It was now raised a good two and one-half feet off the floor, with a large revolving turntable in the center and a lightbulb-lined runway that bisected the audience section. Approximately three hundred orange-and-black seats had been installed, in tiers, and the overall effect was surprisingly intimate, considering the commodiousness of the room. I was informed that Gary Smith, our art director, had designed the modifications, and the attractiveness of this enclosure where it would all happen soon was starting to get to me.

George showed us the control booth and explained it was equipped with the very latest goodies. Then, briskly, he moved out of there and we followed on his heels. I could almost hear his brain clicking as he surveyed the studio from the back row of seats, atop the highest tier. He slowly scanned the stage with slightly narrowed eyes and I knew he was making mental notes, filing away suggestions to the stage crew, instructions to the prop department and the like.

Finally, somewhat reluctantly, we left Stage 43 and headed back for the offices—George in the lead, the Waldmans behind him and Bradford and I bringing up the rear.

"Uh, when do we see Judy?" I asked him.

"She's coming in after lunch," he answered.

"How did the CBS dinner in New York go?"

"What? Oh, great, great."

"How'd they like the parody?"

"The parody? Oh, they loved it. They just loved it. And they loved her, Mel. She was sensational that night. They ate her up."

I nodded and walked along silently.

After a moment, he said, "Why do you ask? About the parody, I mean?"

"I don't know. I . . . just wondered if they saw the humor in it."

Now it was his turn to be silent. Then he looked at me and said, "As a matter of fact, a lot of them did laugh. But I don't think Stanton or Paley thought it was very funny." William Paley and Dr. Frank Stanton were, respectively, the president and chairman of the board of the Columbia Broadcasting System.

"Hmm. I hope to God they didn't think it was a presage of Things to Come."

"What?"

"Never mind."

As we rounded a corner on the third floor, I noticed a door across the hall from the gaggle of Garland offices with a sign bearing my name. Johnny smiled. "That's your office," he said. "Want to take a look?"

He opened the door and I stuck my head in. To my happy surprise, it was a fairly large, reasonably cheerful if rather antiseptic room, with a large, old upright piano, a desk, a drafting board, and even a few prints on the walls.

Johnny looked at me and smile. "Like it?"

"Not bad," I admitted.

"Let's go to lunch."

An hour and a half later we were back in Schlatter's office. He was remarking on how good Judy was looking and how excited she was about the show. The phone on his desk rang. He picked it up, listened for a moment, said, "Thanks," and hung up. He looked at us and smiled.

"She just drove past the auto guard. She'll be up here in a couple of minutes." He grinned slyly. "Hey, let's break her up." He quickly outlined his plan.

She entered the office to find George and Bill Hobin, who

would direct the shows, with their heads together, engaged in seemingly serious conversation. Bradford, the Waldmans and myself were in a huddle, ostensibly discussing music and scripts. The two secretaries were busily typing away, eyes glued to their machines, oblivious of her presence. She stood there, looking at this beehive of activity, not saying a word. George looked over his shoulder at her and said, very casually, "Oh, hello. Just sit down somewhere. We're very busy. We'll get to you as soon as we can." He turned back to Hobin and immediately reengaged him in conversation. Judy looked at them, at us, at the secretaries. She backed out of the doorway, read the "Judy Garland Show" sign on the door, and said loudly, "Oh, thank Christ I'm in the right place. For a minute I thought I'd wandered into the Gale Storm offices."

We all broke up, and there was an immediate orgy of kissing, handshaking and hugging. She was extremely warm with me, embracing me and saying how happy she was to have me to help her. "Gosh, ma'am," I mumbled, "I ain't doin' nothin' any red-blooded, loose-hung, Amuricun boy wouldn't be *proud* to do."

She laughed her musical laugh (E-flat, as I recall) and said, "You nut! When are we going to get together on the music?"

"Gee, Judy," I answered her, looking serious. "I don't think I can make it until"—I looked at my watch—"at least seven or eight minutes from now."

She laughed again and turned to Schlatter. "I can see it's going to be the 'Silly Hour' around here."

George managed to look hurt. "Aw, now why would you want to go and say a thing like that, Min?"

She shook her head, giggling. "I can't cope with this so

early in the day!" I was taking my first really good look at her. She was very thin, thinner than I had ever seen her. She had really worked hard to take off pounds, and the result was startling. She looked years younger than she had when last we met. Her figure had never been notable. She was short, high-waisted, small-breasted, with extremely bony wrists and arms, narrow ankles and undistinguished legs (which, I suddenly remembered, had looked inexplicably great in the "Get Happy" number in MGM's *Summer Stock*). The weight she had stockpiled in recent years had done nothing to enhance her body and had, in fact, aged her appearance.

Now, pounds lighter, she looked more like her old self than she had for a long time. She was dressed in what we would come to recognize as her favorite outfit; white cotton slacks, a light blue and white checked blouse, soft leather slippers and a crumpled fisherman's hat, worn on the back of her head, with the front of the brim pulled down sharply.

We all dawdled over amenities for a time. Then Schlatter suggested Judy and I go off somewhere and get acquainted musically. A rehearsal hall was located. "I've got a lot of music down in my car," said Judy. "Why don't I go down, pick it up, and meet you back here?" I offered to go for her, but she insisted on doing it herself.

"Okay," I said. "I'll be across the hall."

I walked over to my office officially for the first time, tested the piano, which had apparently just been tuned, looked at the prints on the wall (I decided they would have to go), sat down behind my large, gray Formica-topped desk and waited. And waited.

After ten or twelve minutes had passed, I got up, walked to the doorway and looked down the hall. Judy was walking toward me. She was clutching a sheaf of music to her chest with her right arm. In her left hand, swinging loosely at her side, was a bottle of Blue Nun Leibfraumilch.

Little alarm bells suddenly tinkled in my head. I mentally stuffed a pillow against them, and they subsided into a muffled blur. As she walked up to me, she smiled and asked if I had any glasses in my office. I told her no, but that we could look for some. She shook her head quickly, handed me the bottle, put her left hand in mine and said, "Let's go sing."

We found the rehearsal hall easily. Judy quickly walked over to a table that held an empty coffee-maker and, more importantly, a stack of styrofoam cups. She pulled two from the telescoped bunch, uncorked the bottle she had retrieved from me and poured us each a liberal helping of the amber liquid. Though I am fond of an occasional glass with my meals, I have never cared for wine on its own. This is no time to get picky, I thought. I accepted the cup she proffered. She held her drink up in a silent toast, moved it toward her lips and then, perhaps sensing some small concern I might have, she said, almost apologetically, "This television jazz is all new to me. The Blue Lady helps to get my heart started."

I smiled. "So who's asking?"

She closed her eyes, arched her eyebrows and gave a little shrug. "Nobody," she said. "I just thought——"

"Absent friends," I interrupted, raising my cup.

"*Lachiem!*" she answered almost inaudibly, and took a large sip of wine. The Leibfraumilch was chilled perfectly and tasted good. I put the cup down on the music board of the piano. Nodding toward her music folder, I asked, "Whatcha got?"

She walked over to the piano as I sat down, and placed the manila envelope in front of me. She was looking at me, scrutinizing my face. I felt suddenly self-conscious, and I made a great show of leafing through the music, nodding appreciatively as I came across a song I liked. She leaned over the piano, arms folded in front of her, her gaze even more intense. With a small effort, I raised my eyes to hers. "Some good tunes here, Jude."

"Why would you want to take this job?"

Taken aback, I could only muster, "What? What do you mean?"

"Why this job?" she persisted. "I don't get it."

I looked down at my hands for a moment. Then I looked back at her and said, "Well, first of all, I've been in love with you ever since I can remember." (My first half-truth!) "And . . . let's face it, you're the only real superstar around these days. I don't feel it will damage my singing image to write for you. And it will certainly reactivate my initiative to be creative."

"Well put. The language is a little pedantic, but it was well put."

I grinned at her. "Well, the Blue Lady hasn't gotten *my* heart started yet. Give me time, and I'll four-letter-word you to death."

She poured herself another cup of wine and drained half of it. Then, from out of left field, she said, "I think Jack Jones is the best jazz singer in the world."

The pillow slipped slightly away from the alarm bells. I said, casually, "Yeah, Jack's a fine singer."

"No, but I mean, he's not just a fine singer. There are a lot of fine singers. He's the best jazz singer in the world. Don't you think so?"

I knew where this was leading. Jack was and is, in fact, a close friend of mine. He had recently stated in print and on television that I was his favorite jazz-oriented male singer. I was extremely pleased and had thanked him personally. Now I realized Judy had heard him say it or perhaps had read it. She's baiting me, I thought. This is a test. To what purpose?

I decided to play it cute. "Well, now that you ask," I said, putting my left hand to my heart and shaking my head slightly a la Jack E. Leonard, "no, I don't."

"Oh, really? Who do you like?"

"Well, frankly, I favor Ernest Tubbs."

"Ern . . . ? Who the hell is Ernest Tubbs?"

I looked amazed, slightly disgusted. "Look, if you're going to discuss jazz singers, and you don't know who Ernest Tubbs is"—I shook my head sadly—"well, I mean, there's just no point in——"

"You bastard, you're putting me on."

"Now, Judy, don't get salty just because you're unaware of a guy who cuts us all to shreds." I wanted to change the subject. Fast. I picked up a sheet of music. "And now folks, for your dancing pleasure, from the beautiful new Boiler Room high atop the Hotel Martin Bormann, in the heart of downtown Gallup, New Mexico, the Pearl of the Orient, the Mutual Broadcasting company is bringing you——"

"You'd better understand something right now. This is my show. My company produces it." She was referring to Kingsrow Productions, in which she acted as president, with Freddie Fields and David Begelman holding executive positions in the company. "Just remember, you're working for me. And nobody puts me on!"

There was a perceptible edge to her voice. "I'm gonna

get respect around here. It's not going to be like the old Metro days. For once, *I'm* running things." She took another sip of wine. "You know how Mayer used to treat me in the old days?"

"I've heard stories."

"Well, bub, nothing you've heard could begin to tell the half of it. I had to take it then, but not any more." She smiled a tight little mirthless smile. "You want to know something? These days grown men are afraid of *me*. Even my lawyers, my managers. I really shake 'em up. They get out of line, I chew 'em up and spit 'em out!"

She looked up at the ceiling for a moment, then glanced back at me. "How about you, Melvin? You afraid of me?"

The pillow fell down into the pit of my stomach, and the bells were ringing loud and clear, a real four-alarm fire. I took a deep breath. Well, I thought, this is it! It would have been an interesting project to work on but . . .

"Sadie," I began, struggling to keep my voice calm and emotionless. "We have to begin with a premise. The most appropriate one in this case is that you are full of shit." Her eyes opened just a little wider. "I don't know whether you want me to pass or fail this little oral test you're giving me, but I know one sure thing: if I do fail, if I don't command your respect, right here and now, then I'll be worse than useless to you."

"You don't have to———"

"Please allow me to finish. Schlatter didn't just hire me to write special material for you. He wants me to pick tunes with you, to help you be comfortable with every aspect of the musical end of this show. Now, unless you intend to listen to my suggestions and ideas, then I am the wrong guy in the wrong job and about as out of place around here as a bastard child at a family reunion. Period. End of speech."

Her jaw muscles clenched. "Are you finished?"

I leaned back in my chair. "I don't know, Judy, am I?"

She took her time answering. Almost casually she reached around in front of me, took the first piece of music she found out of the folder. Very quietly, she said, "I like this tune. Let's try it."

I felt off-balance. I stumbled through a few keys till we found hers. I played an arpeggio, and she began to sing.

In recent years, I had heard her newer recorded efforts on my car radio, in jukeboxes and at various friends' homes. Her attempts to sing at the top of her lungs had saddened me. Few people can sustain that much volume without impairing their ability to read a lyric properly or maintain their intonation. In Judy's case, it seemed her penchant for belting a song had divested many of her recordings of warmth, musicality and the general sense of the lyrics. Her severest critics had pointed time and again to her wildly wavering vibrato, now in some semblance of control, now totally out of it.

I sat there at the piano, as she began to sing "Mama's Gone, Good-by." And I could hardly believe what I heard. Her tones were pure and clean, the little catch in her voice that I had found so appealing in *The Wizard of Oz* was more evident than ever; her vibrato, as she sang softly and sweetly, was as regular and dependable as a fine Swiss watch, and her intonation at this level of DBs was right on the money. I suddenly felt cold. Then I realized that chills of delight were coursing through me. The hair on the back of my neck actually stood up, and I laughed inwardly as I remembered some movie I had seen years before in which someone had used the phrase, "How do I know it's great? Because the hairs on my neck stand on end!"

So there we were—Garland and I—she, singing her heart out to no one in particular; I, with a large lump in my throat, playing the piano in my fumble-fingered way, swimming in the moon-pool of her voice. She came to the end, held the last note perfectly and let it die away. I shook my head slowly from side to side and said, "Jesus!"

She smiled dreamily, leaned over and kissed me on the cheek. "We'll get along," she said.

I sat there, shaken. Between the little power play she had pulled on me and the superb bijou performance she had just treated me to, I was dizzy with doubts. And despite my bravura attempt to assert my self-respect and define my position, despite her lightning-quick turnabout, despite the kiss on the cheek and the reassuring words, I wasn't even certain I had won a draw in the first round.

Chapter 3

Nearly every television variety show operates in a three-phase pattern. First, there is a preproduction period in which songs are chosen, scripts are written, guests are hired, sets and costumes are designed, musical arrangements are made, rehearsals are accomplished. Secondly, the show is taped in a studio, usually, in part at least, before a live audience. Finally, the show enters the postproduction stage. This is when the credits, titles, cast list and the like are inserted, along with the commercials. At the same time, the program is "sweetened," i.e., prerecorded applause and laughter are judiciously added to the "dead" spots—the little valleys of awkward silence where a joke failed or a song didn't get an enthusiastic enough reaction.

"The Judy Garland Show" now plunged headlong into Phase One.

The creative staff conferred on the subject of "who":

who would we get to function as a foil for Judy, to handle introductory chores on the show, to be funny, to complement our star, to sing a little, dance a little? Everyone had his own idea about who ought to be "who." In the course of a week's time, we met and rejected over a dozen contenders before settling on Jerry Van Dyke.

If a man who is over six feet tall, with stubby blond hair, hulking shoulders, a crooked smile, and a fondness for smoking cigarettes through a long, slender Marlene Dietrich-type holder can be called "impish," then you have a reasonably accurate picture of Jerry. He was ingratiating, charming, funny and talented enough to overcome the stigma of being Dick Van Dyke's brother, especially since Dick was one of the hottest properties in show business and Hollywood wiseacres had openly remarked how Jerry had only gotten the job because we were trading on the power of his brother's name. Jerry, delighted to have been chosen to work opposite The Legend, was naturally concerned as to what his general character and attitude were to be. How did he relate to Judy (at that first meeting he said "Miss Garland"), on the show?

When Johnny Bradford and the Waldman brothers told him one of the lines he would be delivering to her: "What's a nice little old lady like you doing on television?", he smiled a frozen smile. Somewhat later he walked into my office and asked me what I thought of it. I told him I thought it was funny. He didn't think so, and he was worried about it. He was right: I was wrong. We were *all* wrong. In attempting to "humanize" our star we were damaging her image by going on that kind of tack, but we couldn't see it at the time.

In fairness to the writers, Garland howled when she heard the line. In fact, she seemed to be extremely pleased with all the preliminary material. She would come to Television City around ten every morning, whereupon we would go down to the trailer for coffee, danish and a few laughs. The trailer, incidentally, was completely self-contained, with a full bathroom; kitchen; bedroom; living room area, in which sat a small piano, and a well-stocked bar; and all this in air-conditioned comfort. Judy and I worked several mornings in that trailer, while the writers went back up to their offices to fashion the finished script and Schlatter, Smith and Hobin, in their cloister, pondered the first-show guest possibilities.

Judy's choice was no surprise to anyone—Mickey Rooney. All the help he had given her in the beginning—acting lessons, really—from the vast storehouse of his experience, was still indelibly imprinted in her mind. Every millimeter of admiration she had felt for him in the old MGM days had not only remained untarnished throughout the intervening years but had literally burgeoned with the passage of time, like dollars in a savings account, quietly accruing interest. When she had worked in Mickey's Andy Hardy films, he had held the distinction of being the No. One box-office attraction in American films. Now, some twenty-odd years later, she was starring on a multimillion dollar television show and Mickey, who had seen palmier days, needed the exposure (not to mention the guest-shot money).

Judy's loyalty to her old friend and mentor was as fierce and unswerving as was his for her. "But," she confided to me one morning, "that's not why I want Mickey on the first one, Mel. Oh sure, he can use the money, I guess, but he's never in that much trouble. When you're that good you always bounce back, somehow. Mickey's been up and down a dozen times in the last ten years. Means nothing! Just when they're counting him out, he does a *Bold and the Brave* and whap!—everybody flips all over again!" She was referring to Mickey's incredible performance in an otherwise undistinguished war movie. He had improvised a crap-shooting scene in the picture that still stands as one of the classic pieces of film acting.

"No," she continued, "the truth is, I'm a little nervous about this first show. Working with Mick will put me at ease. And," she added firmly, "he'll be damn good for the show."

At that moment I couldn't help remembering Mickey's words about Judy. The rhetoric was almost interchangeable.

The offices were now buzzing with action. More secretaries had been hired. People shuttled from office to office, bursting with ideas, suggestions, revisions. George Schlatter juggled a telephone in one hand and made continuous notes on a pad on his desk with the other. He was stimulated, and his exuberance was contagious.

Especially infected with his virulence were Tom and Frank Waldman. Frank, the older of the two, had the kind of long, lined face and graying hair that you see in Van Heusen shirt ads. He was tall and well set up, and his sense of humor was on the droll side, perfectly counterbalancing Tom, who was shorter, chunkier and bore little resemblance to his brother. Tom was, for want of a better word, sturdy-looking, and his shock of black hair, his open countenance and football-coach physique belied his quick temper. There was never any evidence of sibling rivalry between them, and generally, they seemed to suit each other very well indeed.

The Waldmans, Bradford and I were now real buddies. We swore undying fealty and came within an inch of indulging in a mass wrist-cutting-melding-of-our-bloods ceremony. My early concern over whether I could adapt myself to working for and with others had completely vanished. I was sure the show was going to be a winner. I was positive we would make a real dent in *Bonanza*'s ratings. The writers and I were certain we would all be associated successfully for a long, long time. In one fell burst of camaraderie, we all bought identical Rolex GMT Master watches. They kept lousy time, but that didn't matter. They were tokens of togetherness, badges of belonging. Self-winding fraternity pins for the back-room boys.

Our production meetings were in high gear. Seated at the long table in the meeting room were the cogs that would make the wheels go round. Besides Schlatter, Hobin, the writers and me, on hand were Nick Castle, our choreographer; Gary Smith, scenic designer and associate producer; Ray Aghayan, who would fashion Judy's wardrobe as well as design the show's costumes; Mort Lindsey, our musical conductor, who had also worked as Judy's personal baton-wielder for the past few years; George Sunga, the unit manager, a valuable as well as personable little guy; Jack Elliott, an arranger from the East Coast who would also act as music coordinator.

Though these meetings were essentially concerned with the technical and creative aspects of the show, they were broken up more than once by the unexpected appearance of Judy. She was enjoying her new toy immensely. That's exactly what the show seemed to represent to her, the most wonderful dollhouse anyone ever had, brimful on the inside with talented, "fun" people, who belonged exclusively to her. She loved them and was free to play with them any time she chose to, with no one to interfere. So she would exercise her presidential prerogative over Kingsrow Productions, and when she did, everything stopped. And not, I might add, to the detriment of morale.

Suddenly, in the middle of budget talk, music argot and concept wrangling, here came The Legend into the room. She would smile and say, "Oh, please go ahead, don't let me interrupt," but her infectious presence made continuing impossible. Soon she would be seated at the head of the table, in command, telling dirty stories from an apparently inexhaustible supply until the room was reduced to one continual roar of laughter.

Judy's sense of humor was legendary and her reputation for telling a story skillfully was well deserved. Two examples:

EXAMPLE No. 1.

One day, when she had again seated herself at the conference table, she told us her favorite story, "Shoot Ol' Blue."

"There's this very nervous man," she begins, "who's on the verge of a breakdown. His doctor advises him to get away from the city. 'I have a friend who owns a hunting lodge,' says the doctor. 'Why not go there for a week or so? Get away from it all, do a little hunting.' So this man says, 'Gee, that's not a bad idea. Might do me a world of good.' So, the doctor arranges for his patient to go hunting, and when he gets to the lodge he's met by the owner of the place. Call him"—she gestures wildly in the air, searching for a name—"call him George." (She laughs, and so do we.) "Anyway, this man tells *George*—" (This time she pronounces it "jaw-urge," her head tilted down, looking through her little squared-off glasses at Schlatter, who grins appreciatively.) "—that he wants to go hunting right away, and he asks what kind of game he can expect to find. 'Mostly possum and raccoon,' says George. So the man says to get the dogs and let's get at it. 'Not dogs,' says George. 'Just one. Dog.' He whistles, and around the corner of the house comes the biggest hunting dog *any*one's ever seen. 'That there's Ol' Blue,' says George. 'Greatest huntin' dog in the world. Wait'll you see him in action!' " (George has begun to sound like an accurate impression of Walter Brennan.) "So, they go out in the woods, and in a little while this city guy spots a raccoon. He raises his rifle to shoot, but George stops him. 'You ain't gonna need that,' he says. 'Just keep an eye on Ol' Blue.' Now Ol' Blue takes off after the coon, trees him, wraps his front legs around the tree and shakes it like mad till the coon falls out of the tree. Then Ol' Blue jumps on the coon and fucks it to death."

There is a burst of prolonged laughter from the men at the table. The two secretaries taking notes at the meeting are flabbergasted. They work hard at choking back the laughter but to no avail.

"So, anyway," Judy continues.

"Oh, there's more?" cries Schlatter.

There is another roar, during which John Bradford yells, "You'll never top that last line!"

"Really! Are you finished?" Judy asks, in mock disgust. The laughter trickles away.

"Now then," she begins again, "this city guy's jaw drops, and he says, 'That's the goddamdest thing I ever saw!'

" 'Want to see it again?' asks George.

"The city guy says yes, and in a little while they spot another coon. Sure enough, Ol' Blue trees the coon, shakes it out of the tree, jumps on it and fucks it to death!"

Once again, the room explodes. Judy joins in this time. She is enjoying herself. "Now the city guy says, 'I'll bet he can't do it one more time,' and, of course, that's a challenge George can't ignore. So, they set out again, and it isn't long before they spot another coon. But this time, the coon runs up a very big tree, and no matter how hard Ol' Blue shakes it, this tree won't budge. Well, naturally, George is embarrassed so he says, 'Can't blame Ol' Blue. That tree is just too damn big for him. I'll go climb up and shake that coon outta there.' So, he shinnies up the tree and the coon sees him coming and keeps backing away. Finally the coon climbs out on a limb and George goes after him. Then the coon leaps onto a higher branch, and the one George is on begins to bend, and then splinter and crack and all of a sudden it breaks! And as George is sailing down toward the ground—" (The chuckles are already starting; we can imagine what's coming.) "—as George comes tumbling down, he yells to this city fellah—" (She cups her hands around her mouth like a megaphone.) "—'Quick mister, SHOOT OL' BLUE!!' "

Judy's laughter sails out over the room, louder than the rest. It is fully a minute before we are back to normal. Then she rises, sighs and says, "Well, I've got to go. I hope I didn't interrupt anything." Without another word she heads for the door and exits. Schlatter looks after her adoringly. "She's beautiful," he says, shaking his head in wonderment. We agree. Someone gets a bright idea. We order several blazers from a local costumer, including one for Judy. A few days later we present it to her. She is touched and wildly amused. On the breast pocket of each coat is a yellow jacket patch. Embroidered on it in large letters is the legend: SHOOT OL' BLUE. For weeks afterward, as we walk through the halls of Television City we are each stopped by dozens of people who ask:

"Say, what's with this Ol' Blue business? Is it some sort of secret code on your show or something?"

"Hmm. 'Shoot Ol' Blue.' What's that gonna be? One of the segments on the Garland show?"

"Hey, where can I get one of these 'Shoot Ol' Blue' jackets?"

We jealously guard our little private joke as long as we can. Then, when the meaning becomes generally known, we gradually stop wearing them altogether.

EXAMPLE NO. 2.

Early on, I made the mistake of telling the staff that, while I had no compunctions about my (or anybody else's) use of vulgarities, a specific one that I had a distinct aversion to was the well-known four-letter designation for breaking wind. Whenever any of the Garland staff made use of it, I would wince and say, "For God's sake, you know I hate that word. Knock it off, will you?"

Unaccountably, one whole week went by, and not once did I hear the word uttered. Then one day, the entire creative staff went down to the trailer to finalize the music for the first show. We sat around, discarding this song, penciling in that one. A thought came to me.

"Hey, Sadie!" I said to Judy.

"*Sadie?*" she laughed incredulously.

"Sure. It's better than Frances!"

"You have a point, Melvin."

"Seriously, I just thought of a tune I love."

"Really? What tune is that?"

"Remember a thing you did on Decca called 'Buds Won't Bud'?"

She shook her head violently from side to side. "Oh, no, not that song. *Never* that one."

"You're kidding. Why not?"

She looked me right in the eye and said, quite casually, "It makes me fart."

My jaw dropped down to my chest. For a microsecond I couldn't believe what I had just heard. Then everyone in the room broke up, and I realized I'd been had. From that day forward, that unpleasant little word received the most concentrated usage imaginable in its odoriferous history, from the show secretaries on up to George Schlatter. Needless to say, I had to learn to live with it. I created my own mental Gardol barrier against it, and eventually built up a kind of immunity to it. When the fun had run its course the word disappeared from our daily lives as rapidly as had the Ol' Blue blazers.

There were, quite naturally, a few problem areas as well as periods of enjoyment in those early weeks. Mort Lindsey proved to be a capable musician and arranger. On the other hand, he was becoming a minor thorn in the sides of quite a few people. He was required to be present at the production meetings. When asked to comment on how a specific piece of music should be arranged or at what tempo some tune would lie well for Judy, he knew his business down to the letter. But his long association with her had imbued him with an annoying authoritarianism where she was concerned. He felt he was entitled and obliged to criticize anything and everything that didn't strike him personally as being up to snuff. Consequently he made frequent acerbic remarks about the quality of the script, the dialogue and, on one occasion, a dress Judy was to wear.

Schlatter was patience itself. Whenever Mort would leave the room, there would be oaths of "Jesus Christ!" and "Who the hell does he think he is?" George would say, soothingly,

"Take it easy. Don't rock the boat. Let's get this first show off the ground. Mort'll settle down." Gary Smith agreed. "He's probably as *noodgy* as we are about this first one. I think he's doing what he's doing out of nerves." We all managed thereafter to ignore Lindsey's frequent and irrelevant observations, but more than once I heard someone mutter, "He's a good musician but a giant pain in the ass!"

Mort had chosen a New York arranger, Jack Elliot, to handle the bulk of extra orchestrating that would have to be done as well as fill the post of music coordinator. Where Mort was tall, fairly trim, with a pleasant smile and light-brownish hair, Elliot was of medium height, with thinning hair, a very white complexion and a darkish beard as the day progressed. His arrangements for the show proved to be among the tastiest I have ever heard, full of rich string sounds, humor when that ingredient was necessary or a fat, kicking, swinging big-band noise on the brighter-tempo numbers. He was generally liked by everyone on the show, but he had one small kink. He was rabidly anti-Hollywood, and he made no bones about it. To some New Yorkers, rapping Los Angeles and the California way of living is almost mandatory the minute they step off the plane at L.A. International. And so it was with Jack.

"Man," he would say to just about anyone who would listen, "you *really* dig the scene out here? What a load of crap! Nothing but phonies, smog and crazy drivers. I wouldn't trade a block of New York City for this whole town!" We would nod, hypocritically sympathetic to El-lee-utz Kom-play-nt and let it all go in one ear and out the other. Judy's ear, on the other hand, was something else again. She had had enough discord in her life, and she didn't want or need any at this stage. Since Elliot was very vocal about his disdain for the City of the Angels, it wasn't long before she got wind of it. The information went in one of *her* ears and stayed there. Soon the word got around that she wanted Elliot out. No one ever found out how or why he retained his job, but the best guess was that Mort Lindsey intervened on his behalf and somehow talked Garland out of firing him. That was a lucky save, since, as I have mentioned, he turned out to be a rock; and much of the credit for the glossy orchestral sound the show achieved was owing to his fine composing and arranging.

We all got a little surprise and one of our deepest insights into Judy's personal appraisal of her own professional assets when we suggested doing a rather funny bit built around "Over the Rainbow." She regarded us with pure astonishment.

"You've all got to be kidding," she said sternly.

"Uh . . . no . . . no Judy, we thought it would be pretty funny if——"

"There will be *no* jokes of any kind about 'Over the Rainbow'!" she said evenly. "It's kind of . . . sacred. I don't want anybody *anywhere* to lose the thing they have about Dorothy or that song!"

We then suggested that she at least close the first show with "Rainbow." Again, her reaction was negative.

"Mel, you saw me do it at the Palace. Do you honestly think we could ever match that performance on TV?"

I answered her question with a question. "Does that mean you're never going to sing it on the show?"

She thought about it for a moment. Then, very seriously, she said, "I don't know. Maybe not. If I do, it will have to be for a very good reason."

Judy's precise assessment of the importance of that song

in her life has always remained with me. Some performers go all their professional lives without getting lucky enough to share identification with a song. Conversely, it is a common practice among certain artists to reject their musical signatures, no matter how responsible that song might be for their fame and success. That philosophy is usually accompanied by cries of, "I'm sick to death of singing the damn thing. Besides, that was then and this is now. I want to look ahead, not backward." A guest star on a subsequent Garland show felt that way about his lucky song. But not Judy. To her, "Over the Rainbow" was nothing short of holy, and she regarded it with gratitude and awe.

The first show was to be taped on Friday, June twenty-fourth. Mickey Rooney had been decided upon as the guest. The taping week was scheduled as follows: Monday and Tuesday, general rehearsals in Rehearsal Hall B on the second floor of Television City. Wednesday, runthrough with the entire cast in the same place. Thursday, camera blocking (setting up the video shots and moves) in Studio 43. Thursday night, orchestra rehearsal of all the music with the cast, in addition to any prerecording that might be needed. Friday, rehearsals all day, segment by segment in 43, followed by a dress rehearsal in front of an audience, probably a *kvetch* of little old Jewish ladies with shopping bags, dragged in off Fairfax Avenue in the midst of buying their afternoon groceries. At approximately seven thirty the select invited audience would be admitted. And at eight the premiere Judy Garland television show would get under way.

Monday and Tuesday went very well. The esteem in which Mickey and Judy held each other was a joy to behold. They reminded me of two great bullfighters, preparing to perform mano a mano. Jerry Van Dyke had made great inroads with our girl. She really liked him, and it showed in their dialogue as well as the special arrangement I had written for the two of them, a sort of opening statement of principles built around the popular song "I Believe in You."

Wednesday runthrough, and so far not a hitch. Judy was way, way up. But Schlatter was looking pale and tired. Late on Wednesday, when everyone had gone home, I walked into his office.

"Hey, Melvin," he greeted me wearily.

"Hi, George."

"Gee, it's going good, huh?"

"Yeah, seems to be. Say, pal, are you OK?"

"Me? Sure, I'm fine. Why?"

"You look tired, that's all."

He pressed his temples with his thumb and middle finger, then rubbed his hand down the length of his face.

"Bullseye!" he said. "I am. Tired as hell. Between you and me, I was on the Dawn Patrol last night."

"The *Dawn Patrol*? Hey, dad, it's a great old movie, but is it worth losing sleep over, when we've got such a heavy——"

He waved his hand in the air. "No, you don't understand. The Dawn Patrol. At Judy's."

I shrugged. "Shall I go out and come in again?"

"Look," he explained patiently, "almost every night—or should I say morning—about four A.M., she calls me and I go over to her house. The Dawn Patrol, dig?"

"Four in the morning? What for?"

It was his turn to shrug. "She's edgy about the show. Oh, she's not about to show it around here. But in the wee small hours, it starts to get to her. Anyway, I get up and get over there and we have a few drinks and I hold her hand and reassure her. And believe me, this is a little lady who needs a gang of reassuring!"

"Wow! How does Jolene feel about it?" Jolene was George's wife, a very pretty former model who had appeared for a time on Ernie Kovacs's television series.

"Well, she's not exactly jumping up and down on the bed, clapping her little hands with joy, but she understands. It's important to keep Judy happy. Let's face it, that's part of my job!"

"What about André? Isn't he taking care of that department?" Judy was currently seeing a singer named André Phillipe on a more or less steady basis.

"Naw," George replied. "That's not what she needs right now."

"Final question. How long does this Dawn Patrol jazz go on? Indefinitely?"

"Or at least," he laughed, "until I'm a prime candidate for the laughing academy."

"Well, good luck, coach. Hang in there."

On the way out I ran into George Sunga, our unit manager. He was a perfectly proportioned little man, built along the lines of Alan Ladd, another small guy whose posture and bearing fooled millions of people into believing he must be much taller than he actually was. Sunga had a beacon-bright smile and one of those faces that prompted instant affection from everyone with whom he came in contact. He was highly respected at CBS, a rare tribute to anyone of his relatively young years. Judy had already dubbed him "The Oriental Hatchet Man," and he bore, with tireless good humor, the inevitable Pearl Harbor jokes along with the incessant hallway salutations, viz.: "Ah, good eevering,

Sssunga-ssan, ruvvery to rook onnuh your face." This tolerance on George's part was magnanimous to say the least, since he is of Filipino extraction. I mentioned I had just come from Schlatter's office and that he looked beat.

Sunga nodded. "The Dawn Patrol, huh?"

Surprised, I answered, "That's right. How did you know?"

"Because he's not the only one getting calls at all hours of the night from Judy. If it isn't him, it's Freddie Fields, or Begelman. And when she calls, they go."

Fields and David Begelman were Judy's agents, managers, mentors, and, possibly, lifesavers. In the early 1960s, when her career was in real danger of foundering once and for all, they had taken her in hand and instigated the now-famous concert tour that had completely revitalized her professional life and her bank balance. Begelman was tall, with a prominent nose and two stock facial expressions; total concern and worry or shy, lopsided grin on those rare occasions when everything *seemed* to be going well.

By contrast, Freddie Fields was the prototype agent, sharp, slick and quick. Of medium height, he enjoyed the fact that he bore a rather startling resemblance to Douglas Fairbanks, Jr., and he went out of his way to dress and act the part. He had been a highly successful agent with Music Corporation of America, and he brought to the Judy Garland situation all his years of wheeling-and-dealing experience. He and Begelman had coddled Judy through the problem-laden concert tours. Now, along with Schlatter, they were flying the Dawn Patrol.

"Boy, that's what I call 'guts football.' Up all night and then work all day. How do they take it? Hell, how does *she* take it?" I asked.

He grinned. "You know what Johnny Bradford calls her?"

"No. What?"

"He calls her 'The Concrete Canary.' "

"Yeah," I said, digesting it. "That fits." Just how apt that description was, I would discover in the near future.

Thursday's blocking went well, as did orchestra call that evening. A decision was made to prerecord one of Judy's songs, which she would lip-sync on the show. While lip-syncing is anathema to most singers, it was Judy's particular teacup, thanks to all those years of practice at Metro. Her renowned "mouth choreography"—the trembling lower lip, the tremulous, quivering facial muscles—was brought under control, and the actual mouthing of the lyrics was minimized. This technique is an art in its own right. Very few singers can bring it off, because the tendency is to over-exaggerate the words you are matching; and the result is usually unsatisfactory. In Garland's case, however, the performance was always near-perfect, and I had to watch very closely to perceive any sort of "dubbed" effect.

Late Thursday night, the Judy Garland crew took its leave of Stage 43. We all went our separate ways, secure in the knowledge we were riding a winner. How could we know we were all rushing blindly toward the edge of the cliff? Poor unsuspecting lemmings.

Chapter 4

Friday night . . . June 24 . . . 8:00 P.M. Stage 43 is jam-packed to the back row. The audience is composed of friends, CBS executives and their families, press, television and radio representatives, a liberal sprinkling of big names in the entertainment world. A fine, invisible silver chord of anticipatory excitement pervades the atmosphere. The crowd is rooting for Dorothy. They are all caught up in the web of nostalgia, a pervasive network of memories that serves to entrap every heart and mind in the place. She mustn't fail, she has had too many heartbreaking disappointments throughout her career. This is the biggest chance she'll ever get. So runs the sentiment, thick enough to cut with a knife.

John Harlan, the show announcer, has welcomed the guests. Jerry Van Dyke is announced. He comes out and warms up the audience. The band is tuning up. Everything is in readiness, awaiting only the emergence of our star. Word comes from backstage she is nearly ready. A few CBS execs look at their watches but without great concern. It is only 8:15, not *really* late. Besides, nobody honestly expects the show to start exactly on time. In her dressing room, Garland is having last-minute dialogues with Schlatter. Orval Payne, her hairdresser, casts a critical eye at her, darts in quickly, smooths down a random strand and deftly sprays it, all in one practiced movement.

Judy asks Schlatter whether Cary Grant is in the audience. A week prior to this evening's taping, Schlatter had come up with a clever idea for the beginning of the first show. Opening shot: Judy, on a telephone, saying: "Oh, go on . . . say it . . . please . . . say it just once . . . just for me." Cut to Cary Grant, at the other end of this call, who says: "Well, all right—ready? JUdy, JUdy, JUdy!" Since every mimic within the bounds of memory has employed this phrase when imitating Cary Grant, we all fall in love with the idea. Phone calls are instituted to Mr. G, but he says no, in no uncertain terms. Even a personal plea from Judy herself is to no avail. "Besides, Judy darling, I have never *actually* said 'JUdy, JUdy, JUdy' at any time in any picture I've made! I don't know how it all got started, but it would be a cheat. I'd really rather not!" Judy is hurt by his refusal but graciously asks him to attend the premiere taping. He says he'll try, but he is not in the audience. Schlatter softens the blow by saying he thinks he spotted Cary but is not sure.

Now John Harlan is told we're ready to roll, and he informs the audience, which breaks into spontaneous cheers and applause. The control booth announces over the talkback system that we will roll in thirty seconds. A hush comes over the crowd. There is genuine electricity in the room.

Over the loudspeaker we hear, "Five—four—three—two—one—Roll tape!"

Mort Lindsey gives the thirty-three-piece orchestra the downbeat and the first Judy Garland television show gets under way with the overture of Garland-identified standards that is played at all her concerts. On the studio monitors, we see Judy in a pretaped sequence, dressing, having her makeup applied, her hair done, getting into a car, driving to Television City, walking through the artist's entrance, coming up in the elevator, entering Stage 43 and then making her live entrance from upstage right to center stage, down front.

It is one hell of an entrance. There is wild cheering, whistling, applause, as she stands there, beautifully coiffed, sumptuously gowned, tastefully appended with just the right amount of jewelry, eyes sparkling, looking young and slim. The Aghayan creation she is wearing has a "now" look about it, and her weight loss lends itself perfectly to the slender sheath. She resembles nothing so much as a top high-fashion model. The ovation continues. It is more like a final tribute at the end of a performance than an opening gesture of respect. She is deeply touched. She smiles, and her teeth gleam. Normally they are slightly dull and uneven, but she has slip-on caps that are works of art, natural and becoming.

She opens her mouth wider and begins to sing the opening song, a special arrangement I have written on "Sunny Side Up." The first eight bars or so are lost in the din, but the audience settles down and with characteristic savvy, she belts it across, biting out the words, her vocal tones edged with an excitement that immediately communicates itself to the throng. She is vibrant, in tune, at the top of her form. Everyone senses this, and when she has finished, there is an even greater reaction than at the start.

Now Mickey comes on to strong, warm applause. Together they duet on a parody of "All I Need Is the Girl/ Boy." The audience loves it. Now they both reminisce about the old Metro days, and then Jerry enters the scene. Mickey takes his leave to get ready for his production number. Jerry banters with Judy, delivers the inevitable line, "What's a nice little old lady like you doing on television." The crowd roars, mainly because Judy's "take" is a masterpiece. I shoot a glance at the CBS contingent. The smiles seem forced. Uh-oh, I think, it's "Call Me Irresponsible" all over again.

Mickey sings "Thank Heaven for Little Girls" surrounded by the predictable bevy of female six-footers. He and Judy engage in a talk spot replete with still photos and film clips from some of their old movies. They re-create one of their most famous numbers, "Could You Use Me" from *Girl Crazy*. In the final segment, Judy institutes the "Trunk" spot. She begins by singing a few bars of "Born in A Trunk," from *A Star Is Born*, from behind a large label-bedecked wardrobe trunk. She takes an article of memorabilia from the trunk and tells an anecdote about it. Then she sings a few songs directly connected with what she has been talking about. On this first show, she sings, "Too Late Now," "Who Cares?" and her blockbusting version of "Old Man River." As the last larynx-bruising note of "River" reaches its almost interminable climax, there is bedlam in the studio. These are the strongest cheers yet, a real standing ovation. Flowers are carted to the stage by CBS pages. It all looks and feels and sounds like Judy's opening night at the Palace.

Afterward, there is a party for the cast, crew and invited guests. Judy makes her entrance in about forty-five minutes, and there is another round of applause and cheers, as though it were opening night on Broadway and this is the Sardi celebration after the curtain has rung down. She makes her way through a maze of congratulations to where I am standing.

"Well?" she asks.

"What can I tell you, Sadie. You were nothing short of magnificent."

She preens like a peacock and says, "Yes, I was good, wasn't I," but there is nothing self-loving about the remark. It is, rather, a seasoned artist's realistic appraisal of her work on a given evening.

So went the first taping. We had all worked hard to make it come off. Now a welcome weekend of rest would prepare us for a fresh start Monday on show number two. I collapsed into bed in the early hours of Saturday morning. Like every other member of the staff, I wanted total peace and quiet for the next forty-eight hours. No music, no talk, no decisions, just a nice, lazy, relaxed weekend, goofing off around the house, playing with son Tracy and watching a little television. It was not to be.

Saturday morning's serenity was shattered by the ringing of the telephone. It rang many times. Congratulations from my "fellow woikers" poured in. And of course, I then felt obliged to join in the spirit of things. Sleepy-eyed, I found myself dialing several of my cohorts, lavishing praise upon their heads, basking in the sunshine of their reciprocity. The incessant phone activity ceased around noontime, and I had visions of getting back into bed and pulling the covers up over. But it simply was not to be.

Apparently there was a big difference of opinion between all my associates and "Snow White" (a special nickname by which I referred to my wife). As long as I was up she felt compelled to inform me she really thought the show was lousy, unoriginal and lusterless. She also alluded with a great show of indisputability to a specific dancer she had observed during the taping of the show. She knew that girl was just the type I was drawn to and was sure I was having a tawdry little roll in the hay with her.

I was too surprised to be angry. I asked her to explain just when and how this assignation could have taken place. My job precluded either the time or the opportunity to indulge in extramarital activities. I also reminded her that I had forked out a large chunk of money to buy this ultramodern mausoleum in ultrafashionable Beverly Hills by way of trying to salvage the marriage. She would have none of it. She railed away at me, promising to keep close tabs on my movements. Christ, I thought, I'm married to Superspy. It's going to be furtive-looking trench-coated men ducking into doorways when I turn around, black Mercedes sedans gliding along behind my car, ingenious little "bugs" planted in my office, in the rehearsal hall—hell, in the goddam toilet bowl!

This war of attrition had been going on since the inception of our marriage and was highly corrosive. I was incessantly challenged by my wife on every subject imaginable. I had allowed my sense of values to bend like a willow in the wind in order to keep the peace. But calling black white when every normal instinct in me cried out to call it black, when my brain and heart saw, quite clearly, that it *was* black and battled with that side of me which negated simple truths, was placing my battered mind in a totally untenable position.

And that day, when I had heard enough, had issued one too many unnecessary denials, I fled the manse, hopped on my bike and escaped to the safe, dark confines of a moviehouse. As I rode to the theater, I forced myself to calm down and let my mind wander as much as one can afford to while riding a 250 cc. Yamaha on the city streets.

I chuckled inwardly when I thought of the first time I had walked into Judy's trailer wearing a black leather jacket, carrying a white crash helmet, with a pair of World War II flying goggles around my neck. She treated me to a double take and said: "I see Mommy let you dress yourself today."

I just grinned, straight teeth, crooked smile.

"Now, *really!* Aren't you rushing Halloween just a little bit?"

I explained I was wearing standard garb for motorcycling. She made a rude reference about the state of my mind. "You're going to break your ass on that goddam thing!" she warned me. She also said I would break other things unmentionable.

"Aw, what the hell, Jude," I countered bravely. "Nobody lives forever. It's safer than walking. Did you know that ninety-five percent of all accidents happen in the home? Gee, a feller's got to have a *little* fun."

"FUN?" she practically yelled. "What have you got? Some kind of death wish or something?"

My reasons for cycling were personal and peripherally tied in with my problems at home. Since serenity was the order of the day for Judy, I felt discretion was the wisest course to adopt, so I left her question unanswered. Besides,

I somehow sensed getting too close to her personally would dissipate our professional relationship and weaken my value and position.

But now, as I straddled the Yamaha, the wind cooling the June heat on my face, I recalled the brief history of my zeal for motocycles, beginning with a little putt-putt I had rented a few years back in Bermuda, continuing with the purchase of a fairly tame 50 cc. two-wheeler on my return to California, and right up to the present, having graduated to an honest-to-God "sickle" about eighteen months back. *Time* magazine had recently done a feature article on me and had insisted upon using a picture of me on a bike. The story, to my surprise and dismay, had turned out to be a pungently sarcastic one, and the caption under the picture had read: "He was frighteningly manly." The tenor of the piece was unmistakable; everything I undertook in my life, work or play, had an underlying purpose—I was continually trying to prove my masculinity. I had read the article at the time and shaken my head in disgust. Apparently I had not convinced this amateur psychiatrist *Time* had sent round to interview me that the simple freedom of movement one enjoys on a motorcycle, the joy of being unsurrounded by glass and steel, the fresh-air factor, were the uncomplicated ingredients that contributed the only reasons for forsaking my car most days.

I stopped for a red light. There was one other reason, I admitted to myself. Snow White. She had claimed, publicly and in private, that I was a vicarious individual in the extreme. She had pointed with glee to the fact that I hated to fly yet loved airplanes, that my obsessive movie-going was a perfect example of experiencing excitement without actually placing myself in danger. In short, I was a prime escapist,

who never really *did* any of the things done by others whom
I openly admired.

I waited for the light to change and tried to be introspective. I supposed there was a little truth in what she said. I
was afraid to fly. I had canceled an important television
appearance in the East only a few months back because the
weather was marginal. Two planes had gone down in one
week, and I was scared out of my wits. But, I reasoned with
myself, other people are as afraid of airliners as you. Donald
O'Connor, Jackie Gleason. Movie hero Richard Widmark,
who was once quoted as saying, "I get the feeling every
time I get on a plane, it's going to be my last time, that the
plane's going to crash." I tried to find some comfort in being
a member of that select group, but it didn't help. I *was*
afraid, that's all there was to it, and no amount of rationaliz-
ing softened my shame.

But the motorcycle was something else. I didn't have an
iota of fear about riding it, even though my one-time neigh-
bor, veteran motorcyclist Keenan Wynn, had severely admonished me for driving it on the streets of Los Angeles. Out of
foolishness or ignorance I had ignored his warning, and the
mechanics of handling the machine had become second nature to me. Snow White had grudgingly expressed surprise
and a very small amount of reluctant admiration for my
bike-riding. At that moment, waiting for the green light, I
suddenly realized her endorsement was totally unimportant
to me. So was *Time* magazine's evaluation of my motives.
As the light turned green and I pulled away from the traffic,
I felt a little like Gregory Peck in *The Big Country*. Unob-
served, he had ridden Old Thunder, a wild, unbroken horse,
for the sheer pleasure of proving *to himself* that he could.
My chest swelled with self-vindication.

Now if I could only beat the flying bugaboo.

In the cold light of Monday morning, when our collective ardor had cooled somewhat, the various members of the Garland team met in George Schlatter's office to perform a critical postmortem on the show.

"First of all," began George, "the 'little old lady on television' *shtick* doesn't make it. The network brass hated it." There was a brief moment of disgruntled stirring.

"Also," he continued, "we've got to find a way to keep Judy from touching everybody. I mean, every time she got near Mickey or Jerry she had her hands all over them."

"Aw, come on, George," Bradford interrupted. "That's stretching it a little, isn't it?"

"Maybe. But that's what it looked like to Aubrey and Hunt and Mike Dann." George was referring to James Aubrey, the tall, slim, prematurely gray chief of programming for CBS, who was also known, semihumorously, as "The Smiling Cobra"; Hunt Stromberg, Jr., Aubrey's sublieutenant, and Mike Dann, another network head from the New York office.

"How do we tell her 'hands off'?" Tom Waldman asked. "It seemed to give her confidence, you know—making physical contact like that with the guys."

"Linus and his blanket," mused his brother Frank.

"What?" asked George.

"Oh, nothing," Frank replied. "I just think it's a small point, this 'touching' business. She was a smash Friday night. Why bring her down? Maybe she'll just stop it by herself."

Schlatter was silent for a moment. "All right. Maybe you're right, Frank. Anyway, I'll handle it personally if and when I feel the time comes."

The general consensus was that it was a good, if not great, opening show. It certainly had looked more expensive than it had cost: $140,000. In fact, the single common comment I had heard at the party on Friday night was that the first one had the look and feel of a "special," and there was quite a bit of speculating as to whether the succeeding programs would have that stamp. George Schlatter hoped not. He wisely opined that the only way for Judy to "make it" on a weekly series was to pursue a line of continuity, to departmentalize and create identifiable segments that viewers would look forward to seeing week after week. The "Trunk" spot was one such department. We would have to develop more like it. George then surprised us all by announcing we would not tape a show that week. Judy, he said, was tired, having worked very hard all last week. Also, the little lapse would give us time to reflect upon the fortes and foibles of show number one and attack number two with even greater vigor.

We broke up the meeting late in the morning. I repaired to my office to think. I was to be one of the guests on the second show, along with Count Basie and his orchestra. This one could have very good musical values, I thought. I was determined to write some solid word-and-music sections and derive our strength on this show from those ingredients. I began toying with some ideas at the piano. The phone rang. It was Judy. She engaged me in some small talk for a few moments. Then she got down to business.

"What am I going to sing on the next show?"

"I've just been thinking about that now."

"Don't write anything too complicated to learn. I'm not in the mood."

"Oh? You were in a great mood Friday night."

"Yeah, well that was B.L."

"B.L.?"

"Uh-huh. 'Before Luft.' "

"Your ex giving you trouble?"

'He's not my ex yet. And yes, he's giving me trouble. He's always giving me trouble."

I had met Sid Luft, Judy's husband, on a few occasions and had found him to be charming and likable. It didn't take a great amount of gray matter to surmise Judy was not easy to live with. Two days before, I had decided to avoid discussing my personal problems with her; now here she was, turning the tables, involving me in hers.

Reluctantly I asked, "Want to talk about it?"

She plowed ahead. "He's threatening to go to court. He wants to take the kids away from me. Joey and Lorna. You haven't met my kids yet, have you?"

"No, not yet."

"They're beautiful children, Mel. They're the only good thing that bastard Sid ever did in his life." I made no comment. I had read interviews when Sid and Judy were first married. They glowed with her praise and love for him. When it goes sour, I thought, it really goes sour.

"The thing is," she continued, "I can't put up with the pressure of doing the show and having to hassle with lawyers at the same time. I'm a bundle of nerves over it. That's why," she added, an appeal for sympathy and understanding clearly in her tone, "I thought it best not to do a show this week."

"Of course," I said soothingly. "You don't have to apologize for——"

"Who the hell is apologizing?" she cut in, her voice turned cold and hard. "I don't need to apologize for *any-*

thing to *anyone,* bub! I own this whole frigging shebang, and if I decide not to work until 1971, that's my business!!"

"Hold it, for Christ's sake! How did we get into this in the first place? Everybody around here thinks you were superb the other night, and we're all slightly sorry we're not going to tape this week."

It worked. As suddenly as she attacked, she retreated. "Did everybody in the office really love the show? What did they say this morning? What did George say?"

I decided not to expound too much on the meeting. "George and everyone else is tickled to death about the look of the show, the audience reaction and—hey, you're really fishing this morning, aren't you?"

"Damn right I am. I need a little cheering up."

"All right, consider yourself cheered. You're the greatest. You're the Second Coming, you're the Sermon on the Mount——"

"I'm the National Gallery, I'm Garbo's salary, I'm cellophane."

We both laughed. "Thank you and good night, Cole Porter."

There was a moment of silence. "Feel better?" I asked.

She sighed. "Uh-huh." It was Dorothy at the other end of the phone.

"Right. Why don't you go out and buy a new sable coat or something? It looks like you're going to be filthy rich!"

That really cheered her up. "Will I see you this week?" she asked, almost meekly.

"Sure, Sadie. Let me put some music together, then we can meet and kick around what you'd like to do on the next one."

"All right, honey," she purred, the compleat coquette.

"Oh, and Mel, one more thing."

"Yes?"

"DON'T CALL ME 'SADIE'!!" she screamed into the
phone at the top of her lungs, and hung up. I laughed into
the empty receiver and put it back in its cradle. A small
wave of reaction hit me and churned my stomach. She had
put me through the wringer again. Not a big wringer but
big enough to make me smart all over. What must it be like
for Schlatter late at night, on the Dawn Patrol, I wondered.

I went back to the piano and started ruffling through a
batch of lead sheets. The phone rang again. This time it was
Snow White. She insisted on knowing why I had been on
the phone so long; she had tried to get me three times! I
told her I had been speaking to one of several girl dancers
on the show. They were all down in the rehearsal hall at
that moment, drawing straws to see who would be the first
of several to make it with me on top of my desk during the
course of the afternoon. She spat out one oath and hung up.

For the third time I made an attempt to get down to
work. Again the phone jingled. Snow White revisited. There
followed a harangue not worth repeating here. When I
hung up on her, further concentration was not possible. I
grabbed my jacket and went to lunch.

The next two weeks passed quickly. Before I realized it,
July 7 was upon us, and we were taping the second show.
Since the accent was almost totally on music, Judy was as
happy as a duck in a pond. I had put "The Sweetest
Sounds," "I Hear Music" and "Strike Up the Band" together,
with some special lyrics relating to the Basie band. It was
an extremely effective opener for Judy and the Count's boys.
Judy, with Bill Basie at the organ, sang a quiet, lovely
version of "Memories of You" and the three of us, accom-

panied by the Count's incomparable band, did an arrangement based on Basie's big hit, "April in Paris." The "Trunk" spot fared well, with Judy shining vocally in "A Cottage for Sale," "Witchcraft" and "As Long As He Needs Me" before segueing into her closing theme, "I Will Come Back."

Again, we all met on Monday morning to discuss the pros and cons. The CBS reaction was mostly con. It had been a good enough show, all right, nice singing and dancing, but rather undistinguished considering the time slot in which it would appear. No, we'd have to do better than that if we hoped to throttle *Bonanza*. Oh, and fellas, you've got to get Judy to stop mauling the guests with her hands.

This time, by design or accident, Judy got word of the network reaction. Her boundless enthusiasm during the previous week was sure to be dulled. We expected the worst and were happily fooled when she came bounding in that afternoon with daughter Liza in tow.

Liza was to guest-star on the next show, to be taped on Friday of that week. Judy's eyes sparkled as she introduced her pride and joy to us. Liza was a walking caricature of both her mother and her father, director Vincent Minelli. She had Judy's large and wondrous eyes, her father's nose and slightly receding chin. She also had inherited a great amount of talent and seemed overwhelmed at the thought of appearing on the show alongside her mother, whom she openly adored.

We chatted for a while until Judy asked me what I could come up with for Liza. I told her I had a few thoughts along that line. I also reminded her that she, Judy, was going to do a production number I had built around "Put On a Happy Face." It was to be done with the boy dancers, and the form of it was not unlike her famous "Get Happy." I had played it for her during the week's layoff and she had reacted with delight. Now her face took on a placid, vacuous mien. Her eyes sunk a little into her head as she said, absently, "Oh, I don't want to bother learning that. Give it to Liza instead." Her gay facade crumbled, and at that moment I knew that, within herself, she was depressed and discouraged over the news from the CBS execs. I tried, as diplomatically as possible, to point out I had written the special material for her, and colored my plea by arguing that the lyrics were more suited to mother than daughter.

She wasn't buying. She took a few deep breaths and clicked her mental computer back into "unperturbed." She patted Liza's face. "I'll be down in the trailer, darling," she said sweetly and left my office. Just like that. Liza was a little ill at ease over her mother's sudden departure. Straight ahead, I thought. I went to my piano and played "Happy Face" for her. She loved it, and when she began learning snatches of it, it seemed just right for her. Despite my momentary disappointment at Judy's rejection of the material, I knew her daughter would perform it beautifully.

I wanted to see Judy later in the day, but Schlatter counseled against it. When I reminded him that the following day was Tuesday, that runthrough was the day after that and that so far Miss G. and I had not chosen a single song for her to sing, he nodded, looked away and said, "I know, I know. But today's not a good time, that's all."

"Listen," I asked, "is she all right? Is there anything I can do?"

He shook his head. "No, Bunky, not a thing. She just wants to be by herself in the trailer. She and the Blue Lady are getting reacquainted."

The next day, however, she came to work looking cheerful and happy, as if she had adjusted to any criticism she might have heard. For the opening song spot, I wrote a rather tender translation of "Liza," which Judy would sing while wandering in and around enormous blowups mounted on giant easels. At blocking rehearsal Thursday she saw the pictures, a chronological study of Liza from baby-naked-on-a-bearskin-rug age up to the present. She wept openly as she sang the Gershwin tune, looking at the pictures all the while and shaking her head from side to side emotionally. Liza ran up on stage at the finish of the song and embraced her mother tearfully. There was nothing phony about this overt display of affection. Judy loved her kids actively and passionately and her devotion was returned in kind.

The third show itself was, sadly, a shadow of its predecessors. We simply hadn't found the formula yet, but if wanting to desperately counted for anything, we were all in line for merit badges. Judy sang well, alone and with Liza, Soupy Sales guested fairly amusingly and Jerry provided a very bright cluster of minutes with a hilarious mime-job he developed in concert with an actual episode from an old "Lone Ranger" radio air-check.

During the taping, word came to me that Judy wanted to see me in her little on-stage dressing room. I left the viewing room, went downstairs and knocked on the partition that screened off her cubicle from the audience.

She invited me in and explained she was having trouble hearing the orchestra and the tempos, even though the music was being piped directly to her by means of two huge roll-around speakers. The band was encased in a large, closed-off area far to the right of the performers. There had been, from the show's inception, time-lag difficulties. The tendency to listen to the actual orchestra and not the speakers was ever-present, and the live music was heard a fraction of a second late, resulting in an annoying staggered effect between the artist and the band.

"Do me a favor, will you, darling," she said.

"Of course, Jude. Anything."

"Stay near me on stage, beside the cameras, and bring me in on the right beats."

I hesitated for a moment. This was something I hadn't bargained for. It was one thing to function in an off-stage creative capacity and quite another to be where the audience could see me, waving my hands, conducting Judy, like a personal vocal coach. For the first time in weeks I was reminded of my own status as a singer, and try as I might, I couldn't squelch the feelings of self-preservation that now flooded my senses. Yet, here was The Legend, nervous and worried. I noticed for the first time a small bottle of Smirnoff's on her dressing table.

"Don't worry about a thing, Sadie. I'll be there. Just follow the bouncing ball."

She smiled and squeezed my hand. I left and walked out onto the stage. The audience saw me and began to applaud, apparently thinking I was a guest on the show. I walked to center stage and took a position to the immediate left of number one camera. It was mounted on a small crane, the heaviest, most cumbersome installation in the studio, and since it moved back and forth constantly, I made a mental note to be nimble or have my toes crushed. I heard murmurs in the crowd. So did John Harlan. He came to my rescue.

"Ladies and gentlemen," he announced over the P.A. "We're very proud of the fact that we have secured one of the finest composers in America to handle Judy's special material. You probably know him as one of the top singers in the country, but his writing talent is equally great. Say hello to Mr. Mel Tormé."

The audience broke into warm applause and I looked around, nodding my thanks to them and to John. He knew just how grateful I was for his kindness during those few uncomfortable moments.

I noticed one peculiar, slightly disturbing thing about Judy during the show. She was slurring certain words; no, that's not the correct definition. She was *choking* the ends of some of the lyrics. Almost slack-jawed, she would tail off at the finish of a phrase, and the last few consonants or vowels would come out blurry. When she sang "Come Rain or Come Shine," it sounded like:

> "I'm gonna love you like nobody's loved you
> Cuh rain or come shi . . ."

Her lower lip would curl under her upper teeth, and the ". . . ne" in *shine* would be completely lost. When this phenomenon occurred her eyes would also appear to be slightly glazed. I had a rough idea what caused this, but since I was probably the only one who noticed it (or so I thought), I dismissed it from my mind.

After the taping, Judy disappeared. There was no little gathering in her trailer, no drinks with the cast or crew, no good-night kisses. No Judy. It was perfectly understandable. She had been a good soldier that whole week. She had kept up her spirits for the sake of Liza, and it had no doubt been quite a strain. The Waldmans, Bradford and I went across the street to the City Slicker Restaurant and had a few drinks. We toasted her. And vowed to be wonderfully inventive and original the following week.

And on Monday, true to our words we dove in head first, with the idea of coming up with an idea. There were many between-offices trips, with a hundred different plans discussed and rejected. Late that day, the boys came up with something interesting. One of the reasons Judy had been tapped by CBS for a series was an appearance she had made on the "Tonight" show, months back. She had been witty and articulate. Why not institute a segment on the Garland show called "Tea for Two." It would be a chance every week for Judy to sit with a special guest in a comfortable little drawing-room set, pour tea, trade reminiscences, engage in light banter and, in general, relax for a short time on camera. It sounded good, and they wrote the spot into the script. The first interviewee would be Terry-Thomas, the gap-toothed Englishman whose film roles had made him very popular in recent years.

The other guest was to be Lena Horne, and I was personally excited at the prospect of putting her and Judy together on stage, in a simple setting, and letting them take it from there. No frills, nothing fancy, just a bagful of great songs sung by two great singers. Hey! Interesting thought! What if they paid musical homage to each other. Judy sings Lena's most famous hits and vice versa. Might work! Hmm. Not bad. Not bad at all.

I told my idea to Schlatter and the writers. They liked it, and with the addition of the new "Tea for Two" bit, more than a little enthusiasm was being generated around the office. I went back to my bailiwick to think.

Terry-Thomas. He'll undoubtedly do a monologue. Fine. So much for his solo stint. Now, how to pair him with Judy. Or is that a good idea? Must we forever shove our star into an endless succession of duets with every single one of her guest artists? All right, put that aside for the moment. What about the three of them? Judy, Lena and Terry? Anything there? Perhaps, if I could only find the right piece of material. Thoughts raced around inside my head like a miniature roller derby. I suddenly remembered having done a Noël Coward tome on my old afternoon television series. I jumped up, ran into the writers' office, called Schlatter in and said, "Got a wild thought. Now fasten your seat belts! Judy, Lena and Terry singing 'Mad Dogs and Englishmen.' " There was vigorous nodding of heads, accompanied by "Yeah!", "That's a gas of an idea." Gary Smith, standing in the main office, overheard, concurred and went us one better.

"Why not dress them in Victorian kind of costumes? The girls in very feminine 1890s kind of dresses, the sort of thing they used to wear for afternoon tea in the garden. Women's picture hats of that period were really pretty. Hey, and they could each carry a parasol."

"Beautiful," said George. "What about Terry?"

"Well," said Gary, thinking. "Let's see. Mel, how does that song start?"

"Uh—'Mad dogs and Englishmen go out in the midday sun.' "

"Got it!" snapped Gary. "He's dressed in a sort of old-fashioned seersucker suit, with one of those pith helmets they used to wear in India. You know, the British army-type."

"The kind they wore in *Four Feathers?*" I ventured.

"Right! Exactly!"

"Now that's got to look tremendous! Wait till Judy hears this," I said, turning to George. "What time's she coming in?"

"We're going out there," he answered.

"Out where?" asked Frank Waldman.

"Out to her house. On Rockingham. In Brentwood. She . . . uh . . . she didn't feel very well all weekend. Got a little cold, so she doesn't want to leave the house today."

"A cold? In August?"

"What's the matter? You never hear of a summer cold?" George barked defensively. He looked particularly weary today.

"You been up in those old crates with Errol Flynn again, Major?" I asked.

"What? What the hell're you talking about, Tormé?" he asked irritably. Then he got it. "Oh. Well, you know."

"Yeah, I know."

Midafternoon. We made our way to our various vehicles and set out for the Garland residence. I had taken the Yamaha to the office, and the inconvenience of having to ride all the way out to Brentwood was overshadowed by the sweet breeze and the pleasant smells I encountered on the way.

I was the first to arrive. Judy greeted me with a kiss. She was wearing blue lounging pajamas and her favorite soft-leather sandals. She looked at the helmet. Then she raised my upper lip with her hand and studied the inside of my mouth.

"What're you doing?" I asked.

She peered intently into my throat.

"You can always tell a motorcycle rider," she said seriously, "by the bugs in his teeth."

"You're rotten clean through."

"I know. You're right."

"Deep down inside, you're shallow!"

She laughed merrily. "That's funny. I've got to remember that."

"How's your cold?"

"Come again?"

"Your cold. How is it? Any better?"

"I haven't got a cold, you nut. A cold? In August?"

I did a little broken-field running. "Sure. I figured when you looked in my mouth you were delirious, running a temperature, out of your bird. So, I guessed you had a—you know—summer cold!"

The corners of her mouth twisted up slightly.

"Nice try, Melvin."

"Not good enough, huh?"

"Not nearly."

"Gee, I thought it was pretty inventive on the spur of the moment."

"George tell you I had a cold? That's why I didn't want to come in?"

"Well—yeah. Something like that."

"I like George."

"So do I."

Her tone of voice became matter-of-fact, as she indicated the sofa in the living room. We sat down.

"Frankly, I haven't been able to get organized this last weekend. I had a lot to do, and I didn't get half of it done. So I thought I'd ask you all to come out here and——"

"Nice try, Sadie."

She looked at me with those enormous eyes. "Not good enough, huh?"

"Good God, this is starting to sound like a scene from a Monogram picture," I said.

"With Kent Taylor and Rochelle Hudson," she laughed.

Then she said, "All right. I'm very unhappy about the way
the show's going, and my agents have been on my back for
the last two days about it, and my husband is driving me
right up the wall and André and I had a fight and," she
added, slightly defiant, "I just didn't bloody well want to go
to work today."

"So the mountains come to Mohammed."

She gave me a wry look. "Say, that's a good one. Ever
think of becoming a prophet?"

"Constantly."

"Oh, have a drink and shut up. Where are the others?"

I explained they were on the way. Without getting into
specifics, I assured her we had come up with some new
ideas she would like. She started to pump me about them,
but I put her off. I wanted the staff to present them in force.
When they finally arrived, they explained the "Tea for Two"
plan. She reacted well to it, but something was missing. I
was becoming concerned about her interest-attention span.
Early on, she had had great confidence in the series. Now
nothing seemed to be getting through to her to any degree.
If the minimal criticism the CBS people had offered had
been that debilitating to her, we were in big trouble.

I met Joey and Lorna that day. Joey, eight, was slender,
sandy-haired, with a pale complexion and sad eyes. Lorna,
eleven, was obviously going to be a beautiful woman someday. I could detect nothing of either Sid or Judy in her facial
makeup. Her features were regular, her skin fair and there
was about her a self-awareness of her youthful beauty that
was not unattractive. She enjoyed flirting with me, and we
became friends.

Judy was more interested in showing off her children

than in discussing the coming Friday taping. We all left her house feeling slightly off-center.

Tuesday, when both Terry and Lena arrived at Television City to begin rehearsals, Judy was absent. Someone had called in for her and said she wasn't well and would not be in that day. Terry-Thomas was not disturbed by the news. Lena showed only slight concern. We ran through everything we could without Judy, but it never got very interesting. Early in the day, Lena and Terry were released, and the Garland staff sat about smoking cigarettes and crossing fingers in hopes of good news on the morrow.

On Wednesday, we were once again greeted with a report that Judy could not (or would not) come in. We had a complete runthrough with Judy's stand-in filling in for her. (We had hired this young lady at the beginning of the series to learn Judy's songs and to perform them for her on the first day of rehearsals as well as physically go through the motions on stage Thursday during blocking. Judy would sit in the audience seats, watch her and so become oriented to the marks, positions and moves she herself would have to make.)

Since I could only guess Judy's reasons for not being present, I told Lena, who was a long-standing friend of mine, that Garland had been under the weather, and Lena in turn coolly expressed the hope that Miss G. would be well enough to show up tomorrow, since they hadn't sung a note together yet. Judy, in fact, did show up late in the day on Thursday. She watched the blocking from the rear of the studio, observed her stand-in carefully, but did not attempt the duet with Lena, even though earlier she had greeted that lady with a hug and a kiss.

Lena, the consummate pro, maintained her cool admirably, even singing the duet with the stand-in. But later that afternoon, her fiery temper got the best of her. And when Lena is angry she is even more beautiful, if that is possible. Her celebrated dimples deepen, stunning white teeth flash, impossibly perfect and even, her eyes widen as if she were watching a horror movie and she gets to you. She was hopping mad now, and the target was Judy.

"God damn it!" she cried. "Who the hell does she think she is? We're *doing* this show *tomorrow!* I don't even know if we sound good together. Man, in all my life, I've never seen anything like this. It's the height of unprofessionalism."

It was impossible to argue the point, mainly because it was completely true. To subject people of Lena's caliber to treatment of this kind was unpardonable. There was a little time before 8:00 P.M. orchestra call. On the off-chance she might be there, I went to Judy's trailer. She was. So were Begelman and Fields. She sat in a chair looking glum, drinking Liebfraumilch from a plastic wine glass. I sensed I had interrupted something and started to back away from the door, but she invited me in, saying pointedly that her agents were just leaving. They took the hint and left us alone.

"Have a glass of wine," she ordered.

"No thanks. Look Judy, I know this is none of my business but——"

"Then shut up about it." She was slightly stoned.

"Okay," I sighed. "Let's all go hide our heads in the sand, sports fans."

"Awww. I've hurt the widdle boy's feelings." She waved her hand airily. "Don't be so touchy, Melvin. What's on your mind?"

"Lena Horne."

"So? What about her?"

"What about you?"

"I'll bite, Mr. Bones, what about me?"

"I thought you liked her. I thought you wanted her on the show."

"I do. Like her. Wanted her—want her on the show. So what?"

"Are you putting me on? You haven't sung with her at all. Do you intend to do the opening duet and the medley with her? Not to mention 'Mad Dogs and Englishmen,' which is a bitch to sing and which you haven't even looked at?"

"So? I'll look at it tonight during band call. Jesus, you're a little testy today, aren't you."

"Sure, I'm testy. We all are. We've hardly seen you this week and we're worried. So is Lena. She wants this show to come off."

"Aw, screw her," she mumbled.

"What?"

"I said, don't worry about it. It'll be just fine. I'll take care of Lena." There was nothing more to be said. I got up and left.

That night, everyone was tight as a drum. Lena's outburst earlier in the day was no secret to anyone. What would the confrontation produce? Absolutely nothing. Judy arrived at orchestra call slightly late. She went immediately to Lena, all smiles and loving affection, and charmed the dress off her back. Or so it appeared. Garland was feeling very little pain that night. Not being conversant with the material at hand, she *fumfuhed* her way through the songs, stammering over lyrics, singing many wrong notes. The evening, though not a complete shambles, was far from encouraging.

Next day, there seemed to be some speculation as to whether or not that night's taping would be canceled. Judy had apparently stayed up very late Thursday night. No one knew for sure if she was going to show up. Rehearsals continued down on the stage as if everything was going to proceed normally, but there was genuine gloom up in the office complex. It felt like the bottom of the ninth, last game in the World Series, with two outs, three and two on the batter, the other team leading by four runs and a lot of very quiet people in the home team dugout. Nobody, at that moment, honestly believed we would get a show off the ground that night.

I had a few problems of my own that day. Snow White had begun what I can only describe as an escalation of phone calls that week. It was next to impossible to get any work done. The phone would ring at least once an hour and I would be treated to everything from the latest gossip to interminable interrogation and out-and-out verbal warfare. With that evening's taping hanging in the balance I was not in the proper frame of mind for long-winded telephonitis. I cut short her third call of the day and fled to Schlatter's office.

Not surprisingly, he was on the phone. "Still can't reach her, eh?" he was saying to someone. "Think we ought to send somebody out to the house?" There was a pause as he listened. Then he sighed and said, "Well, let me hear the minute you hear." He hung up. Anticipating my first question he spread his palms upward to the ceiling and said, "Your guess is as good as mine." There was no point in belaboring the subject. She would or would not show. We would or would not tape. Simple, really. I turned to go, and he said, "By the way, Mel, Judy wants you out there on stage from now on."

"Uh-uh, George, no way."

"Shit, haven't I got enough trouble today. Are you going to start getting temperamental on me?"

"Only if you label it temperament."

"Well, what the hell would you call it?"

"I'd call it exercising my prerogative to not perform a service for which I was not hired in the first place."

"Come on, don't split hairs with me."

"*You* come on. Don't cloud the issue. You hired me to write special material for Judy Garland. I have no desire to be a vocal coach, and I think it's unfair of you to expect it."

"Look, you're doing two guest shots on this show in the first thirteen. Now the least you can do is——"

"Hey! Hold it! Am I to understand that's a favor? Charity work? If I'm not good enough for the show as a performer, you should have never agreed to those guest shots in the first place."

He raised his voice now. "Damn it! I didn't mean that, and you know it. I just feel that as one of our biggest assets you should be pulling for the show. You ought to have some rooting interest, that's all."

"Can you honestly look me in the eye and say I haven't shown as much if not more rooting interest in this show than anyone else connected with it?"

"No, but there's rooting interest and rooting interest."

"Hey, George, be sure and forward my mail to my house."

He rose from his desk. "Goddamit, Tormé, sit your ass down and cool off. Jesus! God save me from singers!"

I sat down and said quietly, "We're discussing my writing assignment, not my singing remember?"

"ALL RIGHT! ALL RIGHT!" He came from behind his desk and closed the office door. He sat on the edge of his desk, facing me. "Listen, buddy, this whole show is in a bind. Judy is very unhappy. Our not being able to reach her today proves that, doesn't it? Now, last Friday night, after we finished taping, I had a few drinks with her. And besides saying how happy she was that Liza came off so well, the only other positive remark she made was that, for the first time, she felt sure of herself on stage, because you were there to bring her in at the right place. You have any idea how important that is? To her and the show?"

"Of course. And I think having *someone* on stage, to give her confidence in that department is a fine idea. I just don't want it to be me."

"Why in hell not?"

"Because, Georgie," I explained patiently, "someday, maybe soon, maybe later, 'The Judy Garland Show' will go the way all of them go, to that big cathode tube in the sky. When that happens, I would like to be able to resume my regular career as a boy singer, and with so many producers and directors and singers and movie stars coming to these tapings of ours, all I need is to have them see me, week in and week out, waving my arms on stage, and everyone is going to figure I'm regressing back to the time when I was a vocal group leader. Strange as it sounds, I like to go forward, not in reverse."

"Sure, I know, but——"

"Wait a minute. We're not in disagreement. I said I think it's a great idea. Let's hire somebody to do the job. I'll work closely with him, and the result will be the same."

He shook his head. "No, it won't."

He got up, walked back behind his desk and sat down. "Hey, Melvin, do you trust me? Do you think I'd con you?"

I smiled broadly. "Of *course* you'd con me, pal. You already conned me once into taking this job." I looked around and said to the wall, "Would he con me!"

He flashed a self-conscious smile. "OK, OK. But whether you believe this or not, Judy has come to depend on you. You personally. It's *your* presence she needs out there, not just some guy moving his hand around."

"Look, George, I'm glad she feels that way. It's just that I don't want to be on that stage, in front of an audience, unless I'm performing for them. Can't you understand that?"

He let that slide by. "Will you at least help her out tonight, if we tape? Just tonight?"

I took a deep breath and let it out. "All right. But please, for God's sake, let's not make it a habit."

"You're true blue, Bunky."

"Yeah, yeah, I'm a hail fellow well met, and all that crap!"

Judy arrived in the early afternoon. The day wore on under a large amount of tension. Dress rehearsal was ragged, and "Mad Dogs and Englishmen" was disastrous. There was still talk of canceling the show because of lack of preparedness on Judy's part. But she insisted on going ahead with the evening's taping and even negated a suggestion to eliminate "Mad Dogs" from the rundown.

At dinner break, I have never seen a more disheartened group of people than the cast and crew. Only Terry-Thomas was breezily optimistic and unperturbed. His British reserve served him well, and he remained wonderfully unruffled throughout. In times of stress, mustachioed gentlemen have been known to exhibit a bristling lip appendage. Terry's moustache did not bristle now. If anything, it drooped unconcernedly. A small group went to the cafeteria, but everyone else beelined it over to the City Slicker to fortify themselves with drink before the debacle began.

I went up to my office, closed the door and rested my head on my desk. The afternoon had been tiring. The strain of uncertainty was telling on everybody, and I was no exception. The phone rang, startling me. Snow White, no doubt. I let it ring.

Just before taping time, I went down to the trailer to see Judy. Her little living room was crowded with agents, show personnel and a few well-wishers. We had hardly spoken that day, and when I kissed her cheek and whispered not to worry and good luck, she smiled up at me gratefully. I hated myself a little at that moment. I had been upset with Judy all week. I thought of the inconvenience and anxiety her protracted absence had caused. I was having trouble mustering up any real sympathy, not to mention empathy, for her.

The show begins: Judy and Lena open with "Day In, Day Out." Good. No mistakes, pretty well sung. Lena is brilliant in her song spot, scoring heavily with "I Want to Be Happy" and "Where Is Love." "Tea for Two" is so-so. Judy has not taken the time to become acquainted with Terry-Thomas. She is unsure of herself, even while delivering prepared questions. She touches him a lot. He saves the spot somewhat by being very amusing. Suddenly, we're into the Judy-Lena medley. Everyone holds his breath. Unbelievably, it works very well. Like the clutch hitter she is, Garland pulls it out of the fire. There are audible sighs of relief. "Mad Dogs and Englishmen" is no better than dress rehearsal. Judy blows much of the lyric, but it has a good look to it, and Lena and Terry more than make up for Judy's inadequate contribution.

During the show, perhaps because I worked on the stage as we taped it, I noticed something that was to become a rule, not an exception, throughout the complete run of the series. The audience was heavily populated with homosexuals. A few weeks prior to this, I had heard someone remark, "Judy? Yeah, she's the Queen of the Fags!" I had known for many years that the Odd Fellows had a predilection for La Garland. A minty singer I knew had once told me that the "Madame Crematon" number Judy had done in MGM's *Ziegfeld Follies* was "The Faggot's National Anthem." They were here, in the studio, a fairly large contingent of them, rooting for their gal, and when she closed the show in the "Trunk" spot with "The Man That Got Away," they led the cheers and applause.

When Judy began "I Will Come Back," I walked off the stage and sat down in a folding chair near the band enclosure. As soon as tape stopped rolling, everyone ran out of the control room to congratulate her. Spirits were high, praises were flowing freely. As I sat there, dog tired, Bill Hobin, the director, came over, slammed me on the back and said; "Wasn't she great? Wasn't she just great?"

He was a stubby little man, with wavy black hair, a barrel chest and regular, open features. In 1963, he must have been in his midthirties or early forties. His moon-faced countenance made it difficult to guess his age, and when someone told me Hobin had been having a running gun-battle with booze for years, I found it hard to believe. None of the ravages of hard drinking were evident.

I looked up at him. Bill had been on the wagon for a

long time. Tonight he had fallen off, and who could blame him? The strain of the day had been too much. However, I was not going to be a party to hypocrisy. I shook his hand off my shoulder. "Oh, sure," I yelled at him, "go ahead. Tell her how great she is on one day's rehearsal. And then next week, if we're lucky, she'll show up ten minutes before we tape."

His brows knitted together, and he looked at me questioningly.

"What's wrong with you?" he asked slowly.

"Bill, am I crazy, or aren't you, yes and all the rest of the guys, the people who were cursing Judy for not putting in any time on this show? Now, because her natural instincts and talent pulled her through, is she suddenly supposed to become the heroine of the piece?" I took a mental step off the soapbox. "Jesus!" I said wearily. Hobin looked at me for another moment. Then he patted my shoulder and walked away, toward Judy.

The fifth show is hardly worth mentioning. Since Judy once again elected to remain away from Television City most of the week, that program, taped on the thirtieth of July, was a study in mediocrity, despite some excellent moments provided by guests Tony Bennett and Dick Shawn.

The following Monday morning, I stepped off the elevator on the third floor of Television City and asked the receptionist if Schlatter had come in yet.

"Oh, yes, Mr. Tormé," she said, pointing with a pencil toward the archway. "I just saw him go down the hall toward the gentlemen's room."

I thanked her, went through the arch and turned right instead of heading for the office. George was not in the men's room. I proceeded farther down the hall till I came to a passageway that ran parallel to ours on that side of the building.

George was part way down the hall, dressed in slacks and a cardigan sweater, jiggling a knob on the candy machine.

I walked up to him and said, "Morning, George. What's happening? Is Judy coming in today?"

The candy bar came crashing down into the receptacle. He picked it up, began to slowly peel off the wrapper and without looking at me said, very quietly, "I really don't know, Mel." He took a small, absent-minded bite out of the bar, swung his head toward me, and said, "You see, I've been fired. And so has almost everyone else!"

I had two rapid reactions. The first was no reaction at all, like a second or two after you have been in an auto accident, when your mind refuses to acknowledge what has happened; it just doesn't seem possible. Then, like the thousandth-of-a-second flash of a strobe light, in my mind's eye, I had a quick impression of lemmings going over a cliff. And as I stood there, watching Schlatter deliberately chewing away at that candy bar, a mirthless, half-smile on his face, it dawned on me that "The Judy Garland Show," like some ancient steam locomotive whose engineer has just leaned out of the cab to find the trestle ahead has been washed away, had come to a grinding, screeching halt.

Chapter 5

"Why?"

The question kept rolling around inside me, nagging, persistent.

I couldn't get anything out of George at that moment. He was sleepwalking, out of it, like a man who has been hit a mighty blow in the back of the skull and is in shock. The office staff was a carbon copy of Schlatter, all whispers, teary eyes and open mouths. I walked into my office and sat down heavily. In a few minutes, Johnny Bradford came in. His dark circles looked even darker today. He, along with the Waldmans, had also been dismissed. Hobin would finish out his contract on the first thirteen, then he, too, would go on his merry way.

Bradford grinned at me. "Pretty wild, huh?"

I shook my head. "It's beyond me, John. It doesn't make any sense. We've barely begun to——"

"It makes sense to CBS," he cut in, philosophically. "The show's not what they want. We haven't made Judy come off. So . . . ?" He raised his hands ceilingward, resignedly.

"Oh, come on," I countered, "Do you really think we've been given a fair chance?"

"Yes," he nodded, "I really do."

"Johnny, a lot of shows need time to find themselves. Look at the Van Dyke show."

I was citing the case of Dick's early dilemma with his television series. He had taped many shows that had aired with poor rating results. The program had been in imminent danger of cancellation, when it squeaked through by the hair of its chinny-chin-chin, because they had finally found the formula to make it go. Why not give the Garland writers and producer the same chance?

"Because," explained Bradford, "the Dick Van Dyke show doesn't cost $140,000 a crack and it isn't in the critical time slot we're in." I still felt the firings were premature and basically unfair, and I said so.

"What are you griping about?" he said wryly. "You haven't been fired."

"What am I supposed to do? Run up the flag?"

"You're supposed to do your job, pick up a check every week and run like a bandit."

"And what about you guys?"

"None of us will starve. We'll all do fine."

"You sound like you're glad this happened."

He grunted. "Let's not go crazy. Nobody likes to get fired. But maybe it's for the best. I've hardly seen my family in over a month. I've been alternating with Schlatter on the Dawn Patrol."

"Oh, fine."

"Yeah. Well, at least I'll catch up on my sleep now. And maybe my kids'll stop calling me 'Uncle Daddy.' "

"What about your contract?"

He grinned. "It's run-of-the-show, baby."

"So?"

"So I sue!"

"Who?"

"Oh, CBS, Kingsrow Productions, I'm not sure at this moment. This is all pretty new."

The Waldmans came in. They were alternately hurt and hopping mad.

"What a crock!" said Tom, the firebrand of the two brothers. "We never even got out of first gear!"

Frank, who looked like a successful trial lawyer, soothed him.

"Patience, little brother, better days ahead." He looked at me and said, "Well, kid, looks like you're left holding the fort."

"Or the bag!" amended Tom.

Johnny laughed. "Ah, ah. Judy always spoke well of you, Thomas."

"Listen!" said Frank jauntily. "Why don't we three exiles clean out our desks, go across the street to the Slicker and toast our dear, departed jobs?"

Johnny and Tom nodded their agreement. Halfheartedly, Frank said, "Er . . . want to come along, Melvin?"

"No," I said, "you guys go ahead. I want to sit and stew for a while."

When they had gone, I reflected. They hadn't seemed to really want me along. They now shared something that excluded me. I tried, at that moment, to put a gauge on my emotions. It wasn't easy. I was confused, angry, rebellious.

The writers, I thought, will be okay. There's always a demand for good writers. But what about Schlatter? This had been his big chance, what he had worked for, for a long time. Now he was out in the cold.

I suddenly found myself unaccountably hungry. I started to go to lunch (at 10:45 A.M.), when Gary Smith walked into my office. Later, Gary would go on to produce the teen-oriented television series, "Hullabaloo." Almost overnight, he would change his mode of dress from the conservative suits he once wore to the right-now-with-it styles popular with the younger generation. To complete the picture, his curly hair would grow even curlier and longer until one day he would be the picture of sartorial splendor, according to the doctrines laid down by Bill Blass and John Weitz; but this was 1963 and Gary had not yet busted out. His medium-tall, thin frame was tastefully covered by something soothing from a careful New York haberdasher as he placed one well-polished shoe on my piano bench. He was smoking one of his little cigars, trying hard to look as if he hadn't swallowed a small, yellow bird.

"Terrible thing, huh?" he ventured.

"Not terrible. Stupid."

"You know," he said casually, "I'm being moved up to 'producer.'"

"Well—congratulations, Gary."

"I won't lie to you; I'm excited about it, but I'm also terribly unhappy over George and the boys."

"Why wasn't I fired, Gary?"

"Gee, I don't know. I mean, I have a pretty good idea why, but I don't honestly know for sure."

"Why do *you* think they didn't let me go?"

"Well, because you're writing some great things for Judy, and I figure they think you'd be hard to replace."

"There are a lot of good special-material writers in this town. They could snap their fingers and fifty of them would come running to take my job. No, I can't believe——"

"Bob Lewine wants to see us in fifteen minutes. Why not ask him yourself?"

"I'll do just that."

Bob Lewine was an old friend of mine, who also happened to be a transplanted eastern executive with CBS. I shook hands with him as Gary and I entered his office a quarter of an hour later. Bob, slightly balding, dressed conservatively in a tasteful charcoal-gray Brooks Brothers suit, motioned toward some chairs. He was related to composer Richard Rodgers, and, when I had done my CBS daytime variety show out of New York, we had become friends, sharing an admiration of Rodgers's work in general and, in particular, a preference for the Rodgers and Hart score to an old Al Jolson film, *Hallelujah, I'm a Bum*. Snow White and I had been seeing Bob and his wife socially since they had moved to California. Today, however, there was no small talk. He came right to the point.

"Well, fellows, we're all upset about what we have had to do. But we found it necessary, believe me. Now it's up to you to pick up the pieces and go on from here."

Gary nodded his agreement.

Bob looked at me.

"Why wasn't I fired?" I asked him.

"You want it straight?"

"Is there any other way?"

"Aubrey wanted you out as well. Nothing against you,

Mel. He just felt you were part of the Schlatter regime, and he wanted to make a clean sweep."

"So? What stopped him?"

"Judy. Naturally, she's extremely upset about all this. She and her agents have been fighting this decision all week-end. We finally got her to see it our way. There's too much at stake to allow personal feelings to interfere. But she raised hell when we mentioned firing you. She's adamant on that score."

Gary chimed in. "I told you. She depends on you. I don't think we'd have a chance of continuing if you were out of the picture."

I let that sink in. After a moment, Lewine said, gently, "Well, what do you think?"

I took a deep breath. "I think," I said, "you are all out of your bloody minds! Look, I don't know how effective Schlatter has been as an executive producer, but I can tell you this; if you think Judy depends on *me*, wait'll you get a load of her without George around to keep her happy. Don't you see, Bob? He's got her confidence. And, with all due respect to Gary, without George around, I think you can kiss this show good-by!"

Gary jumped in with, "You're right, Mel, you're right. We've got to keep her happy."

"That's why," explained Bob, "we're bringing in a new executive producer."

"And who would that be?"

"Norman Jewison."

Jewison was a Canadian television director who was just beginning to enjoy some small prominence in films. *In the Heat of the Night* was several years in the future, but I was surprised to hear he was taking this job, since he had made it known throughout the trade that he did not care to be involved in television anymore.

The prospect of a new creative team did little to allay my skepticism. Lewine seemed surprised I wasn't taking the firings in stride. Without actually settling anything, I went back to my office to think. Gary came in and gave me another it's-all-for-the-best pep talk. I must admit I was hard put to understand my own reaction to the situation. Here I was, the only writer on the show to be retained in a mass purge, and I was feeling resentful about it. I wanted to be with my buddies across the street, sharing their common plight. Involuntarily, I glanced at my Rolex. Gosh, guys, I thought. What a shame we won't get to room together next semester.

I picked the phone up and called my manager. I told him how I felt. He left the decision to stay or leave up to me and assured me I was free to quit if I so decided. I hung up. That call was a big help, I thought. Restlessly, I got up and paced around the office. There was a knock on the door. I called, "Come in," and Schlatter entered the room. He seemed composed and resigned, even in a good humor.

"How'd your meeting go?" he asked.

"Swell. Just swell."

"Well, it's up to you now, Bunky."

"Yeah, that's what Lewine said."

"Listen, nothing's changed. One squad goes out and another comes in. That's show biz, pal."

"That's bullshit, buddy."

"Sure, it's a little of that too. But," he sighed, "if you can't take the grind, then don't play on the team."

"That bit of homespun philosophy from Mother Schlatter's Family Almanac is brought to you by the makers of——"

"No, seriously, don't let what's happened make any difference to you. You've been writing some beautiful things, which makes me happy. Remember, you were my idea, and I was right."

"Well, don't worry, George," I said. "The only difference it's going to make is that I've just decided to quit."

He looked concerned. "That would be foolish, Mel. Judy has to have someone from the old guard"—he shook his head and grunted—"the old guard," he repeated wonderingly. "Anyway, if you quit, the show will never get back on its feet. You know, I talked to the lady this morning. She's really broken up about all this. She admitted she was disappointed in the first few shows, but she said she was sure we would find the 'right combination' for her. She was cursing Aubrey up one side and down the other." He lowered his voice. "Between us, she's not fond of Gary. I don't know, I think it's chemical or something. Now if you quit, and the only remaining member of the original gang is Gary, she'll crack after a couple of shows and that will be that."

I looked at him, curious. "Why should that make any difference to you at this point?"

"Because," he explained, "none of this is Judy's fault. And despite all my hard work down the drain, and the plans I had shot to hell—yes, and even those nonstop nights at her house with no sleep, I love the crazy broad. She's a great talent, and she deserves to have a big hit television series."

I grinned at him. "Gee, thanks, coach. I needed that. I know we can go out there and beat those guys now!"

"I'm serious. Don't abandon ship now, Mel. It's not sinking, it's just a little low in the waterline."

"George, you have a gift for imagery. I'm not going to pretend to understand this turn-the-other-cheek attitude of yours, but I have to admire you for it. If I were you I'd be mad as hell right now."

"Oh, I am, I am! I'm peeing blood, believe me. But there's no sense being mad at the wrong people."

"I suppose it's dumb to ask if you have any plans at this moment."

He nodded. "Yep, it's dumb."

I ran out of things to say.

"One more thing," said George. "Gary told me what you did for me in Lewine's office. You know, there's not a hell of a lot of loyalty in this racket, and I want you to know how touched I am. Now don't be embarrassed by what I'm going to say. You're a big talent and a stand-up guy, and there ain't too many of them around. Now how does that grab you?"

"What can I say? I'm embarrassed, Bunky."

"No, *you're* Bunky. I'm George, remember?"

"Oh, yeah, now I've got you pegged."

"Hey, buddy. I appreciate what you did today. I'll never forget it."

We shook hands, and he walked out of my office and away from "The Judy Garland Show." His rise from that humiliating defeat to his position as executive producer of the top-rated NBC behemoth "Laugh-In" is a tribute to his tenacious determination to overcome adversity. However, I find it a source of amusement and an interesting commentary on show business in general that from that day to this writing, George Schlatter has never once offered me employment either as an artist or a writer on a single project with which he has been associated.

Despite the countless pieces of advice I received in the next few days, I continued to be indecisive about staying or leaving. I hated to think of myself as a deserter, but I knew better than to believe for a moment that I, or anyone else, was even remotely irreplaceable. A close associate of Judy's, who has asked to remain anonymous, finally clinched it. In an hour-long phone conversation, he enumerated countless reasons why I should remain with the show. When I explained my position and belief that any one of several writers could easily fill my shoes, he admitted this to be true. His main plea was on a personal level. Judy liked me, and with my recent confreres gone, she would need my friendship and help more than ever. I capitulated.

Judy herself had not called because she had escaped to New York. I learned she and André Phillipe had come to a parting of the ways, and coupled with the firings, it had been considered wise to take a long hiatus, during which she could shop, sup and play in Manhattan. About a week after I had agreed to stay with the show, my manager and I had a meeting at CBS in order to renegotiate my deal. Since I was now committing myself to the run of the show (my earlier employment was predicated on a trial basis), and my singing activities would be severely limited for God knew how long, I had decided to test this new-found indispensability of mine by asking for a considerable increase. There was almost no resistance to this demand, or, for that matter, to our insistence upon a guarantee of four more guest shots within the framework of the second thirteen shows. Then we came to an impasse over my actual duties. CBS and Judy's representatives insisted I continue to work on the stage with her, bridging the gap between the orchestra and Garland. I refused. I offered to work with anyone they hired to fill what I thought of as "that ignominious position." That wasn't satisfactory. They pointed to the new deal we had negotiated. They had acquiesced to all of my requests. Now it was my turn to give. This stage of the bargaining lasted the longest.

Finally, out of fatigue or boredom or both, I achieved what I told myself was a workable compromise; I would work on stage with Judy, but it was clearly understood by all that this was a concession, a *favor*, not to be spelled out in my contract as part of my job. It was childish of me. They had gotten what they wanted, yet I felt I had rescued my self-respect by granting them this special service of mine as a reluctant gift.

Since the show would not resume production for several weeks, I accepted a two-week engagement in San Francisco at the Hungry I. It was enjoyable to be singing again, and in addition, I contracted to write a large batch of new "station promos" (identifying musical vignettes), for radio station KSFO in that city. My work on the Garland show thus far had sharply increased my facility to compose, as well as my desire to do so. I agreed to produce the recording session at which these promos would be taped some time in November, said session to take place in Los Angeles.

Snow White and Tracy came up to San Francisco for a weekend. The very beauty of the city contributed to a temporary surcease of hostilities, and for once, it was fun to be a family, riding the cable cars, walking through Golden Gate Park and enjoying Fisherman's Wharf. Tracy sensed the easing of tension between his mother and father with that fine-tuned sensitivity of the very young, and he proceeded to have the time of his life. I was sorry to see that weekend pass; but I knew instinctively the cease-fire was confined to the Bay City, and I was not expecting miracles to occur back in Los Angeles.

Judy was having a field day back East. Her name was constantly in the gossip columns, dating so-and-so, dining at such-and-such. Whoever handled her press at the time was doing a good job, seeing to it no leaks sprung about the show's problems. Schlatter's release was handled diplomatically, as if his departure had been effected by mutual consent. I could just imagine The Legend in New York, scene of her greatest personal triumphs, playing the gay dilettante, the toast of the town, days full of shopping, lunches, business meetings; nights on the town, going to the theater, with a late snack at Jilly's, exuding largesse and good grace, singing for the noisy pseudo-hip patrons seated around the piano bar. She loved New York, and the feeling was mutual.

I returned to Los Angeles the last week in August and enjoyed the luxury of inactivity for ten days or so. The Garland show was to resume production after Labor Day, with the first taping to take place on Friday, September 13. Judy had returned from the East, and one night just prior to our going back to work, she called and invited me to dinner at her home. She expressly asked that I come alone, and of course, Snow White raised the roof, with insinuations followed by accusations. I smoothed the situation over as best I could, got into my little Corvette and headed for Rockingham Drive.

I noticed, when I arrived, a burly man in the driveway, who held up his hand like a traffic cop, stopping me short.

He walked over to the car, leaned his massive head inside the open window and scrutinized my face.

"Oh, it's you, Mr. Tormé," he rumbled. "Miss Garland's expecting you. I'll park your car." Something new has been added, I thought, as I got out of the 'Vette. I wondered why.

When she greeted me at the door, I asked about the security man.

"Oh, him. Sid's been threatening me again. I feel safer with that guy around."

Something smelled delicious and I said so. She laughed and led me by the hand into the kitchen. I took a good look at her, since I hadn't seen her in weeks. She had gained an almost imperceptible but not unattractive amount of weight during her eastern sojourn. She wore a simple cotton dress, with little makeup, and fashionable low-heeled shoes. She looked fine, I decided.

"You look fine," I said.

"Thank you," she said, curtsying.

"New York agreed with you."

"It always does. I hope you like beef Stroganoff."

"Love it. I didn't know you could cook."

"Buster, there's a lot about me you don't know."

"Like for instance?"

"Like for instance, I'm in love."

"Ah hah! I thought I detected a rosy glow. Who's the victim?"

"*Victim?*" She raised the wooden spoon with which she was stirring the Stroganoff. "I'll club you, you monster."

I held up my hand, Dave Garroway style, and said, "Peace. I apologize. Who is the lucky man?"

"An old beau of mine. Glenn Ford. I dated him a long

time ago, and we've found each other again. Isn't that great?"

"Uh—yeah, I guess so. If you think it is."

She made a strong affirmative motion with her head. "I *know* it is! He's beautiful, a really lovely man. Do you know him?"

"No, I've never met him."

"You will. You're gonna love him."

"Couldn't I just like him?"

She looked at me and shook her head back and forth. "Aren't you ever serious?"

"Not about Glenn Ford, Sadie."

"I've needed someone like him for a long time, Mel. Someone strong. Every woman needs that, even if she won't admit it."

"I got the impression you didn't like strong-willed guys. Like Sid, for instance."

"He," she said darkly, "was something else again." She did not elaborate. "George Schlatter was strong," she said, almost wistfully.

"Don't look back, Jude. That's over with."

With characteristic sudden vehemence, she exploded, "God, I hate that fucking Jim Aubrey! Don't you?"

"How can I hate someone I don't even know."

"Just look how he's screwed things up, firing every-one——"

Dangerous ground, I thought. Choose your next words carefully, Tormé.

"Listen," I said, "I've done a lot of thinking on that score, and I've come to a few conclusions. Want to hear?"

"Go on," she said, eyes slightly narrowed.

"Okay." I began ticking off points on my fingers. " 'A,'

CBS is pouring big bread into this show of yours, right? 'B,' for whatever reasons, Aubrey or Mike Dann or somebody up there didn't like George or the way things were going on the first five. 'C,' they want you—no, they're *dying* for you to be successful, so 'D,' like it or not, they made the move because they thought it best for the show. Now those are the facts of life, babe, whether we like them or not!" I wasn't honestly sure I believed any of the foregoing, but I felt it was what she needed to hear.

She cocked her head. "Now, can the crap and tell me what you—you personally, really think."

I waited just the proper amount of time. "I think," I said, "that part of what I've just told you is whistling in the graveyard. I also think a great deal of it, the biggest part of it, makes some kind of sense."

I changed the subject. "Where are the kids?"

"They've gone out to dinner with their father." She grinned. "Lorna sends her love. She's got a thing for you."

"Yeah, I know."

"Don't you dare defile my baby, you dirty young man."

"Please. I've got enough trouble being Jewish."

Dinner was excellent. I had skipped lunch that day, and I ate wolfishly. Judy pecked at her food, preferring to fill up with wine. Over dessert she said, "By the way, they told me how you felt about quitting. I wouldn't have blamed you. But I want you to know I appreciate your staying with the show."

"It's my financial pleasure."

She shook her head. "I know better than that. You did it for me." She was slightly drunk. She held her arms out to me. "Come over here and give me a big kiss."

My stomach churned. This was totally unexpected. And

it was remotely possible she was after something more than an innocent, platonic kiss. My mind raced. I appeared to consider her invitation. Then I slowly shook my head. "Nn-n-o, I'd better not," I said, as if it were a decision I hated to make. "I'll enjoy it too much, and so will you, and we'll get into a lot of trouble together, and Snow White will find out and so will Glenn, and he'll forget he's not in front of the cameras and gun us both down, just like he did to Brian Keith and Barbara Stanwyck in *The Violent Men,* and then———"

She reached over and clapped her hand over my mouth. "All right. All right, already. You and your goddamned movie mania!"

"Don't knock it, Dorothy. That's where I first saw and fell in love with you, in a moom-picture house."

"Some love," she grunted. "Won't even give me a little nothing kiss."

We lapsed into embarrassed silence. I thought, this is when she is volatile; slightly inebriated but in control of her faculties—easily angered, more easily offended, touchy, haughty, just plain dangerous. I was surprised to find I was at a total loss for words. I broke into a fine sweat, waited for her to make the next move. She drained her wineglass, stared at the tablecloth, drunker than I had realized and said quietly, "Go home."

For a moment I considered trying to mollify her, to mend this tattered little scene. Instead I shrugged, got up, said, "Thanks for dinner," and headed for the front door. As I opened it, she yelled from the dining room, "You bastard! You're really going, aren't you?"

I turned to face her as she came toward me. "Well, what

the hell do you expect me to do? Break out my toothbrush and stay the night?"

She put both hands on my arm and pulled me away from the door.

"I don't want you to go!"

"JUdy, JUdy, JUdy," I said, doing my best Cary Grant imitation.

"Please don't leave me alone," she entreated. She seemed suddenly frantic. "I don't want to be alone tonight. Joey and Lorna won't be home for hours. Stay with me, please. We can watch television or talk or whatever. Just don't leave me alone."

She pushed the door shut with her foot and dragged me back into the living room. For the next few hours we talked. Or rather, she talked. I listened. As she became progressively drunker, so did her verbosity increase. Trying to understand her while she was in this condition was like trying to decipher a code message being played backward on a tape recorder. Sentences ran together, words were slurred to the point of incomprehensibility. Here and there, snatches of sense broke through. Her unceasing hatred of her mother, whom she blamed for most of her troubles, since it was apparently she who had pushed and prodded all the little Gumm sisters into the life of slavery known as show business. David Rose now came in for his fair share of invective, as well as Louis B. Mayer, one of her favorite topics of rancor. She wept great tears as she spoke of the exploitation she had endured while under contract to MGM. Racking sobs shook her body as she repeated over and over again how she had been underpaid and overworked at "The Factory," as she called it, while her pictures had made millions for Metro. There was little point in trying to discuss,

no less debate, these stories with her. She rambled on com-
pulsively, unintelligible at times, while I listened, nodded
my head and continually glanced at my watch. Once she
caught me checking the time. "Whassa madder? You inna
hurry 'r somethin'?"

"Well, it is getting late, Judy, and I——"

"So wha's keeping ya? Go home. Getthehellout!"

This time she didn't stop me as I went out the door.

A few days later, I stopped in at the office to meet the
new staff. In addition to Norman Jewison, on hand were
the new writers, Marvin Worth and Arnie Sulton. Ernie
Flatt, whom I had known from Garry Moore days, had replaced Nick Castle as choreographer. In addition, Bill Nichols and a young Canadian, Bernie Rothman, had been
hired to help with the writing chores. Jewison made a little
Knute Rockne-type speech, expressing his faith in us all and
his long-standing admiration of Judy. The gist of his remarks
was, simply, that we were lucky to be associated with a star
of such magnitude, and he was confident we would avoid
the mistakes made by our predecessors (except I had no
predecessors on the show!).

Later, in his office, we talked.

"Hey, this is going to be fun, working together," he said.

"Thanks, Norm," I replied, noncommittally. "It's good to
see you again."

"Yeah. Been a long time. Since that last TV special in
Toronto, right?"

"Right."

He lit a cigar, offered me one, which I declined. "I ran
the first few shows yesterday," he informed me.

"And?"

He leaned forward, his tone confidential. "There's not a

goddam thing wrong with those shows. I don't get it. What happened?"

"You know as much as I do. CBS wanted Schlatter and the rest of the guys out."

"Hmmm. What about Gary Smith?"

"What about him?"

"Can he do the job? As producer?"

"Well, he was associate producer from the very beginning. I would imagine he'll work out very well, providing he gets some cooperation."

Jewison affected a surprised look. "What are you talking about? Of *course* he'll get cooperation. All he needs. It'll be coming out of his ears!"

"No, I mean, from Judy. If she's willing to dig in, work with him—"

His jaw tightened determinedly. "You leave Judy to me. I'll handle her."

"Norm, how well do you know her?"

He sidestepped neatly. "We're gonna get this show running like a well-oiled machine. Watch and see."

I took a shot at what was on my mind. "And just when you do, you'll be busting out, right?"

"I don't get you."

"It's no secret you've only signed for eight shows. Then you're off and running elsewhere. If you are, by some magic quirk of fate, the guy who can get this train on its tracks, you are obviously going to jump off just as it's going downhill, picking up speed."

He enjoyed the analogy. "Sure, but by that time, it'll be home free, running itself. On schedule, on time, no problems."

"Doctor," I said, "there ain't no such thing as 'no problems' around here. As an old pal, let me warn you; you get starry-eyed about Judy and think you got it knocked, this whole setup will blow up in your face. What we got here is a pretty sick patient, no matter what you thought about the first few shows."

"No kidding. Tell me about it." He looked interested as he leaned back in his chair and waited.

I had put myself on the spot; there was no turning back. "OK," I said, "maybe you're putting me on. Maybe you already know. And maybe I'm talking out of turn. But on the off-chance this might be of some help to you, here goes. Judy is the essential problem, as I see it. She came into this show full of p. and v. Schlatter dazzled her with fancy footwork and she do-si-doed right along with him. Now he's gone, and she's looking like mad for another crutch. Right now, you're it. I'm just wondering what's going to happen when you take off and the floor falls out from under her again. Because believe me, I may not know much, but this I'm certain of: no one will ever get this show to run 'automatically.' The whole *mishigoss* revolves around Judy Garland, and she is too insecure to take her associates for granted."

"So it comes down to the 'care and feeding' of Miss Judy, huh?"

"You just won yourself a cheap cigar."

He shrugged. "That's too bad. But there's nothing I can do. CBS had to twist my arm to get me to do the few I'm doing. When they're finished, I want out."

"That's what I figured. It'll be interesting to see where we go from there."

By way of an answer, he held his hands in the air. It wasn't going to be his problem, at least not for long.

I got up to go. "You know, Norm, I was surprised you took this job at all, even for a limited period of time. What was the incentive?"

He smiled a broad, cherubic smile. Contentedly, he informed me, "They're paying me $100,000 for eight shows. Any questions?"

Chapter 6

"The Judy Garland Show" now entered its second stage of production. There was an aura of vitality and interest around, but I regarded the new setup with caution. I was determined not to be pessimistic, yet I could not help but feel we were batting on a sticky wicket. Judy's deportment under the second regime was an unknown quantity. At best, she would be erratic, of that I was certain. Could I and the rest of my colleagues instill in her a kind of team spirit, a desire to turn this sow's ear of a show into a silken purse? Only the passage of a little time would tell.

We quickly proceeded with show number six. Judy's guests were to be June Allyson and Steve Lawrence. Since she admired Steve's singing and because I knew she had been friendly with June during her final days at MGM, I felt reasonably sure Garland would react well to both artists, and that the prospects for a good show were better than

average. Recalling Schlatter's dictum regarding depart-
mentalizing, I created a new song spot from which I hoped
we would get a great deal of mileage. It was called, "Be My
Guest," and I planned to write new lyrics every week,
tailor-made for each new guest artist to appear on the show.
Judy came into the office on the first day of production,
heard the song and sparked to it at once. Good, I thought.
She likes it. She's interested. Onward and upward. Ernie
Flatt came up with an exciting routine for the opening of
the show. Judy, June, Steve and the boy dancers would do
a production number around "Life Is Just a Bowl of Cher-
ries." Judy and June would dominate the "Tea for Two"
segment that we had decided to retain from the previous
format, and the two girls, along with Steve, would do a
medley of songs associated with both June and Judy during
their Roaring Lion years.

As the week wore on, I got to know the new writers.
They were generally nice guys, with an apparent ambition
to see the show succeed. Jewison was spending a good deal
of time charming Judy, and, from what I could see, she
seemed to succumb to his attentiveness.

Sultan and Worth, two experienced television writers,
were walking on eggs. Their output on this first show in the
new cluster followed a middle-of-the-road motif, nothing
too startling or cloying or funny or sad or flamboyant or
drab or, for that matter, original. They were investing their
talents very carefully, then sitting up in the grandstand,
watching the action with practiced eyes.

Bill Nichols's contributions were professional and creative, but the Canadian lad, Rothman, was a question mark.
He had written special material on a number of CBC shows
in Toronto, presumably under the aegis of Norman Jewi-

son. I have always assumed it was Jewison who created Rothman's job on the Garland show. Rothman was an introverted, selfless young man with genuine talent, but from what he brought into my office by way of possible material for the show, I had to surmise he was not ready at that time to undertake the writing of a major network television show. I worked hard at encouraging him, but little of his songwriting saw the light of day on "The Judy Garland Show."

Wednesday runthrough looked pretty good. We all indulged ourselves in some pretaping optimism. Thursday was looking even better. The chemistry between Judy and her guests was working, no doubt about it. We were all so sure we had a good one going that no one blinked an eye when we realized that taping day was Friday the thirteenth. Instead, Jewison took the fact that it was my birthday as a good omen.

Judy and June had been behaving like the Bobsey Twins that week, all girlish and giggling. It was heartening to see our gal in such good spirits. On Friday, those good spirits were amplified with even more good spirits, courtesy of the Blue Nun Company. Early in the day, Judy broke out the goodies and June, eager to keep the gaiety going, matched Garland sip for sip. By dress rehearsal they were hilarious with laughter.

By show time, forget it! Steve Lawrence observed all of this with astonishment. "Hey, Mel," he said, openmouthed, "we're taping a show tonight! Or are we?"

I assured him we were and that, in spite of how things looked at the moment, it would be a good one. Perhaps because it was my birthday, I allowed myself to do a little wishful thinking. At least Judy had rehearsed all week. She knew the songs and the dialogue. June was so patently in awe of her that her unabashed worship could work to our advantage. Steve was a thing of beauty, professional and prepared to his fingertips. Now if Sadie could only stay in control of the Leibfraumilch . . .

Happily, she did. She seemed delighted to be working again, enthused over her guests, the songs, the chatter. Since it was the first show after a longish layoff, the audience, many of whom we came to recognize as "regulars," gave her an enormous sendoff. "Be My Guest" clicked and seemed a delightful way to musically welcome Steve (and future guest stars) to the show, and when Judy sang "San Francisco" in the "Trunk" spot, the crowd roared. The only mishap of the evening occurred after the taping was completed. I was standing in my normal position beside the center camera when out came June and Judy, well in their cups (no pun intended), carrying the biggest cake I have ever seen, singing "Happy Birthday" to me! I couldn't suppress a face-stretching grin as I walked forward to acknowledge their greetings and the applause of the audience. And then they dropped it! Suddenly the whole stage was a mess of white frosting, splattered crumbs and mashed candles. The audience laughed its collective head off, and I joined in. It seemed a fitting climax to a buoyantly affectionate evening. The stage hands managed to salvage better than half the cake and it was enough to feed the cast, crew and audience!

The CBS brass were patting themselves on the back. The changes they had instigated were for the better. This *had* been a good show, and their faith in their own judgment had been more than vindicated. They told us so that evening and again on the following Monday. So far, so good. Next: show number seven, with Donald O'Connor guesting.

Judy's esteem of his work was only exceeded by her respect for Mickey Rooney's enormous talent. On this show, the writers suggested we use "Born in a Trunk" as a running gag throughout, first with Judy and Jerry Van Dyke, later with Judy, Jerry and Donald, and finally, as usual, with Judy herself closing the show with the "Trunk" spot. I wrote new lyrics to "Be My Guest" for Judy and Donald, and after considerable *noodging* I convinced Judy to do a song I had always been on the hook for called "The World Is Your Balloon," from an ill-fated Broadway musical, *Flahooley*. This she did, with Jerry and Donald joining the singers and dancers to perform one of the most charming production numbers we ever attempted. Jerry repeated his sidesplitting "Lone Ranger" turn, Donald and Judy chatted with true rapport during "Tea for Two," and though she touched him constantly, it didn't matter. For her closing song, The Legend trotted out another of her hydrogen bombs, "Swanee," and bedlam was the order of the day. This show was the strongest to date, so strong, in fact, that a decision was made to air it as the first show in the series.

Judy was high for many reasons that night. In addition to a fine performance and a successful taping, Glenn Ford was on hand. I met him in the trailer. He sat on the couch, looking like an obedient little boy as Judy paraded back and forth, accepting congratulations from the myriad well-wishers who crammed the tiny enclosure to shake her hand or kiss her cheek. As Glenn engaged me in conversation, I got the impression that here was a man dedicated to eternal youth. His appearance had always been boyish in films. Now I discovered his personality matched his looks. As we talked his face lit up with enthusiasm at the mention of Judy and the show. I couldn't help remembering his excellent performance in *Teahouse of the August Moon*. He played a role in which everything he saw or experienced was of unbearable, supreme delight to him. That's the way he was acting tonight, like a college boy who was enjoying a rare privilege, an enormous treat. He spoke of Judy reverentially, grinning constantly, punching my arm with affection. When everyone had cleared out of the trailer, I hugged Judy, added my own congratulations to the long list and said good night. Glenn got up, shook hands with me and said, "You know, I like you."

"Thank you, Glenn. I like you too."

He clapped his arm around my shoulder and said, "No, but I really mean it. I really like you."

Judy smiled. "He really likes you, Melvin."

"Uh, yeah, well, I really like you too, Glenn. And you too, Sadie." (At this point in the conversation, I was tempted to dig my toe into the carpet, blush and mutter, "Aw, shucks!")

Glenn clapped his hands together, his eyes lighting up. I half-expected to see a balloon emerge from the top of his head, with a glowing light bulb inside. "Hey!" he cried excitedly, "Let's all get together some night and go out!"

Judy laughed. "We will, darling. We will. Good night, Mel."

As I was heading home that night I thought; well, sophomoric though he appears to be, he's obviously good for Garland. She was happier tonight than I've seen her in a long while.

Sadly, she showed little interest in the next show. Perhaps it had to do with the guests, since she felt they were not of the stature of a Donald O'Connor, June Allyson or Steve Lawrence, and therefore a letdown for her. She barely rehearsed that week; and when we taped the show (Friday, September 27) a pall hung over the studio, and the resulting performance was lifeless and dull.

Two days later, Sunday, September 29, the first show (with Donald O'Connor), was aired. The following day, Orval, Judy's hairdresser, came up to my office to say that Judy wanted to see me. I entered the trailer to find her sitting at the coffee table, a batch of newspapers spread out in front of her. She rose to greet me, a wide smile on her face. She looked better at that very moment than I had ever seen her. She was dressed in an expensive black sheath, her hair freshly styled, with very little makeup on. She was positively vibrant.

She indicated the papers. "Have you seen them, honey?" she chortled delightedly. "Have you seen the reviews of last night's show?"

I hadn't, and I said so.

"They're absolutely sensational! The critics loved it!"

"Judy, that's great. I'm really happy for you."

"For us! Be happy for all of us."

"All right, for us. But mostly for you, if you don't mind."

Her mood changed abruptly from exuberance to contemplation. "You realize what this means, Mel? The show's going to make it. It's going to be a hit." Tears formed in the corners of her eyes. "I've got something to hang onto now. I'll never be alone again. I've got the show, and you and Glenn and the kids, and"—she laughed suddenly—"I think I'm going to be terribly rich!"

I was about to comment on this, but she pressed on. "I deserve it, after all these years in the business," she said, more to herself than me. "People think of me as a sort of First Lady of show business." Her eyes lit up as she remem-

bered something. "Oh, look!" she cried, as she took a telegram off the piano top and handed it to me. It read:

> CONGRATULATIONS ON A WONDERFUL SHOW LAST
> NIGHT. KNOW IT WILL BE A BIG HIT IN THE COM-
> ING SEASON.
>
>   JOHN F. KENNEDY

"Isn't that marvelous? What a wonderful man. And so
attractive. Did you know he called me from the White
House a few months ago, just to ask how things were
going?"

Before I could answer, she was off on a new tack. "You
know something?" She affected a pregnant pause. "I'm
decent! There isn't a great deal of decency in the world,
especially in our business, and I'm one of the few really
decent ladies around."

How does one answer that? I did not even try. I just
nodded.

Show number nine was highly significant, and a good
example of what motivated Judy Garland. First and fore-
most, she had to be *interested.*

As time went on, we discovered a hard truth. Involvement was impossible for her unless she felt it was worth the
effort. Show number nine was, we learned. The prime guest
was to be Barbra Streisand. Though she had not reached
the heights of superstardom she now enjoys, she was, nonetheless, hot, important, new, exciting, greatly gifted and,
more pointedly, her singing style had been compared to
Garland's. I had never met Barbra, but rumors about her
abounded. She was temperamental, she was unpredictable,
she was foulmouthed, she was nuts. She was also one helluva
singer, and Jewison, in particular, was rubbing his hands

together in anticipation of the Battle of the Century between the two divas.

Norman was looking a little down at the heels these days.
Though the first few shows had been promising, his noc-
turnal duties at Judy's house were getting to him. Perhaps
he had deluded himself into believing it wouldn't be as bad
as I had painted it, the early-morning emergency calls, the
patient tolerance necessary to withstand Judy's grinding,
all-night filibusters, the days on end without a decent night's
sleep. Now, though his mode of dress was impeccable as
usual, his general demeanor was raggedy-ass. I think he
secretly hoped Streisand would give Judy her musical comeuppance and take our Living Legend down a few pegs.

On the first day of rehearsal for this show, Judy called
me. Not from her home. From the trailer. Early in the
morning, yet! I went down to see her. She was playing
Streisand's record of "Happy Days Are Here Again" on a
portable phonograph. She took the arm off the record, invited me to sit, and said, "Listen." Then she began to play
the record from the beginning again. As Streisand's voice
came through the speaker, Judy started to sing "Get Happy"
in counterpoint to "Happy Days." The result was electrify-
ing, one of those chance discoveries in which two great
songs jell into one extraspecial opus. Only the bridge, or
middle part, needed reworking.

"Do you think Streisand will like it?"

"She'd be out of her mind if she didn't."

"I know, but after all, 'Happy Days' is her song, and she
might not——"

" 'I have suffered many tragedies, none of which ever took
place.' "

"Meaning?"

"Meaning, why worry till we present it to her. I think she'll love it. And since 'Get Happy' is one of *your* biggies, she should be flattered you're willing to sacrifice it for a duet."

"Okay," she said, still not convinced. "I guess we'll just have to wait and see." I walked away from that little meeting feeling that, for the first time since I had known her, Judy was concerned over the competition.

Streisand came into my office later in the day to choose some keys and decide what her solo spot would contain. She was very quiet, very friendly, very Brooklynesque.

"Lissen," she said, discussing her selection of songs, "the whole thing shouldn't be a total loss, I think I'll do 'Down with Love.' It's a terrific arrangement. Awright?"

"So why not?" I laughed. "If not you, who?"

She looked at the ceiling and said to the light fixture: "He's a nut. A regular nut. Like me." She looked back at me. "Am I right?" She sat down beside me and got interested in the music. This was as good a time as any.

"Hey, I want to show you something."

"What? What?"

"Since you sing in any key, try 'Happy Days' in this one," I said, as I began the introduction in a key suitable to my range. As she began to sing it, I joined in, a la Garland, with "Get Happy." Barbra kept singing as she half-turned to me, a wide smile on her face. When we finished she exclaimed, "That's terrific! I mean it! Your idea?"

"Nope! Judy's!"

She was even more delighted to hear it had stemmed from Garland. She confided to me that she had been excited and nervous ever since she had been signed for the show. The sole reason was the prospect of working with Judy Gar-

Donald O'Connor with Judy

Judy and Lena Horne each sang the songs the other made famous

Memories of *The Wizard of Oz* with Ray Bolger, "the old scarecrow"

A song and dance sequence with Ethel Merman and Shelley Berman

A talk with Peggy Lee

A duet with Barbra Streisand

Judy in a "Born in a Trunk" closing spot

With Jerry Van Dyke early in the production of the show

The "yellow brick road" leading from Judy's air-conditioned trailer dressing room at CBS, Television City, Hollywood

Judy in a solo moment

Preparing for the Christmas show with Liza Minnelli and Jack Jones (seated), her children Lorna and Joey, and dancer, Tracy Everitt (standing)

"Tea for Two" with Terry Thomas

Martha Raye, Peter Lawford, and Judy

In a pensive moment during "Born in a Trunk"

Judy and Mickey Rooney

With conductor-arranger Mort Lindsey

With executive-producer No. 2, Norman Jewison

Guest star, Liza Minnelli, and her mother

Judy and Mel Tormé

Judy in clown make-up on the final show

land, whom she adored. Groovy, I thought. One more problem solved. When Judy and Barbra met, it was instant warmth, and I knew Garland would be on her toes all week to keep pace with this extraordinary girl.

A fascinating coincidence also occurred on that show. The secondary guests were two young men who had been making a lot of noise on the college concert circuit, the Smothers Brothers. Their act consisted of playing the guitar and bass respectively, and doing humorous renditions of folk songs. They were fresh and funny, but Judy couldn't or wouldn't react to their brand of what she termed *"goyishe* humor." They had been signed for two guest shots, and when this first one had been completed their manager nearly went crazy trying to get a date for the second. He never did. The brothers threatened to sue but never followed through. They did enjoy revenge of a sort a few years later. When the Garland show finally folded, the Smothers Brothers took over her time slot and proceeded to make some kind of television history with their no-holds-barred, tell-it-like-it-is format. (If one can say that a specific time period on a specific network is jinxed, then nine Sunday night, CBS, is that slot. Tom and Dick Smothers tangled with CBS ideology once too often and got chopped at the height of their popularity. Next came Leslie Uggams in a variety format. *Bonanza* proved too much for her, and that show folded after thirteen.)

The complete cast assembled in the rehearsal hall on Wednesday for runthrough. There was enough relish in the air to spread on a hot dog. Judy walked through the opening number lackadaisically. There was polite applause from the sidelines. Then she and Jerry, Barbra and the Smothers Brothers did "Be My Guest." Pleasant. The Smothers went through their segment to appreciative laughter and generous applause from the singers and dancers, who had no trouble relating to them. Then Barbra stepped front and center. Judy leaned over and whispered in my ear, "Now *that's* a Sadie! Let's will the name to her."

"Down with Love" was a bombshell, an intricately worked out potpourri of songs that started down here, built to here, and ended way up there at the top of the excitement range. The kids hooted and whistled and cheered, perhaps a little too vociferously. They were sticking the shaft into Judy a little. Many of them felt she deserved it. While they had come in day after day, working their behinds off, she had, for too many shows, as far as they were concerned, dogged it. She had either been late for rehearsals or not shown up at all. She had been unprepared and unrehearsed more times than not. To those hard-working singers and dancers, she had been unforgivably unprofessional, and they had made no bones about it on several occasions. None of them were worried about the consequences of such outspokenness. Good singers and dancers are at as much of a premium as are honest television repairmen.

Judy exchanged a bit of written banter with Barbra. They sang their "Get Happy"/"Happy Days" duet, and the gang clapped loud and long; but so far Barbra was well ahead on the applause meter. Even a later duet they engaged in seemed a letdown after Streisand's impressive solo spot. Then, in the trunk spot, Judy unfurled "You Made Me Love You" (re-creating the "Dear Mr. Gable" recitative she had originally spoken in "Broadway Melody of 1938"), followed by "For Me and My Gal," and then finally unleashing "The Trolley Song." She laid it down, infusing it with all the heart-catching excitement she could summon, and damme! if she didn't pull it off, planting her feet firmly in that famous performing stance of hers, her arms coming down sharply at intervals to punctuate a lyrical strong point, vibrato in total control, enunciation letter-perfect, intonation flawless, vocal quality loud and clear. It was a performance for her cast, quite unnecessary and yet extremely important, a point of honor, a reaffirmation of her prowess as The Queen. Sure enough, just as she began, "—with his hand holding mine, to the end of the line," the room came to its feet, and it was New Year's Eve. Streisand was clapping and whistling. So was I. With a small, self-satisfied smile on her face, Judy made a tiny bow of acknowledged homage, and walked out of the rehearsal hall, leaving a wrung-out group of performers to ponder the inestimable power of our Lady Leader.

One sour note was sounded during this week. Ethel Merman was to be the "Tea for Two" conversationalist. The idea was for her to appear as a surprise guest, seated in the audience during the taping. Judy would spot her as if by chance and invite her up on stage to participate in the talk spot. Merman suggested it would look funny if she merely went on the show to talk, that the audience would expect her to sing at least one song. Jewison informed Garland, who hit the roof.

"Doesn't she realize this is a weekly feature on my show? And that she's supposed to be coming up on stage spontaneously?"

Norman explained Merman did understand, but insisted on singing something anyway. Judy looked at him for a moment, and said, offhandedly, "Then tell her to go fuck herself!"

"Judy——" began Norman.

"I mean it," she shouted. "Tell her I said, 'Go fuck yourself!' "

"Aw, come on, I can't——"

"Do you want *me* to tell her?" asked Garland evenly.

Jewison shook his head and said unhappily, "No, no, I'll handle it."

"Good!" she crowed triumphantly.

Somehow Norman managed to butter up Ethel and pacify the seething Garland, and when "Tea for Two" was taped, with Merman *and* Streisand gabbing with Judy, the result was a delightful hen party.

With Judy's runthrough performance still dazzling us, the staff was afraid she had shot her bolt and that the actual show would be a letdown. However, she attacked the taping with even more vigor. The result was one of the few memorable shows in the series.

Remembering her good vibrations with Mickey and June Allyson, we contrived to book another pair of alumni from the old MGM era, this time "Scarecrow" Ray Bolger and Jane Powell. Judy had remained fond of Bolger through the years, and I was personally delighted at the prospect of working with him. Toward that end, I wrote a long, intricate arrangement, weaving together many songs based on girls' names. The idea was for the singers and dancers to beg Bolger to sing his big hit, "Once in Love with Amy." He would decline, saying he was tired of doing the same old song, and he would then launch into the medley of "girl" songs, explaining how he would be quite content with "Laura," or "Margie" or "Diane," *anyone*, as a matter of fact, except old Amy, who was getting on.

I played the arrangement for Jewison and the writers, who agreed it was the strongest piece of material I had written thus far. When Bolger heard it, it was obvious he hated it. I had heard from many quarters how irascible he could be, but I had felt confident he would like what I had done. Instead, he fumed and fussed.

"Jesus!" he spluttered, "I've been watching the show and you've been writing some good stuff, Mel. I was sure you'd come up with something original for me. Not the same old 'Amy' crap!"

Jewison, as taken aback as I, gently tried to point out that this was *not* "the same old 'Amy' crap" but a new approach toward squelching the "same old 'Amy' crap." He further indicated that Ray had not been active in the guest-shot television area and that alluding to "Amy" would be extremely valuable, since Bolger was so closely identified with the song. Not to be swayed, Ray stubbornly stuck to his guns, and I think Norman and the rest of the staff were as gloomy as I over his rejection of the material. Then, inexplicably, he walked into my office the next day and offered to do the medley if I "modified" it. I had conditioned myself to abandon the idea. Now, suddenly, it was back on the board. I thought briefly of matching Ray's obstinacy and insisting the medley be performed exactly as I had written it; but there is scant time in the right-now pattern of television for temperament, and I agreed to prune it.

Snow White and I had been arguing fiercely during this period, and she had placed me "in Coventry." The silent treatment was much to my liking, far less corrosive than the endless verbal fracases, on top of which my office phone was blessedly quiet. Without warning, during this show, she came out of her shell and began to bombard me with calls again. This condition was to continue for the run of the series, and the maddening part of it was that, in most instances, I was in the untenable position of being the mute recipient of her invective, owing to an office full of staff members.

The Bolger-Powell show fell somewhere between good and mediocre. Everyone worked well and "Tea for Two" was particularly nostalgic, with Judy and Ray reminiscing about *The Wizard of Oz*. Because Bolger was the first guest we ever had who had been in "Oz," we once again prevailed upon Judy to sing "Over the Rainbow." She refused to consider it, but compromised by singing and dancing with Bolger to a song that had been cut from the final release print of *The Wizard of Oz*, namely, "The Jitterbug." Judy had spoken to me of this song and explained how disappointed she was when it had been cut because of the length of the film. Now she resurrected it, and it was a high spot.

This proved to be Jerry Van Dyke's last show. He had expressed discontent for some time now. Originally hired as a kind of subhost, more and more in recent weeks his role on the show had been minimized to the point of scant participation. "If this keeps up," he groaned to me one day, "I'll be able to take that giant leap from comparative obscurity to total oblivion." The tenth show was his undoing. So many years have passed that, while I am grateful for a reasonably retentive memory in the writing of this book, a few details are fogged by the passage of time. I have searched my mind for the details of his departure. Was he fired or did he quit? The answer is relatively unimportant. I was sorry to see him leave, another of the "old guard" gone West.

Steve Allen and I guested on the next one. We had gone to high school together back in Chicago, had played in the same band in the Windy City and had remained close friends throughout our lives. Steve's wife Jayne shared "Tea for Two" with Judy, and Steve sang a duet-medley with her, a group of songs from his Broadway musical *Sophie*. For my part, I was enjoying some unexpected success in the form of a hit record, a pop-rock tune called "Comin' Home, Baby." I sang it on this show, surrounded by beautifully gowned girl dancers and ten white motorcycles. Judy and I harmonized "The Party's Over," and, taking a leaf from her Streisand "Happy Days"/"Get Happy" book, I handicrafted an ambitious medley, more than fourteen songs, which Steve, Judy and I sang in twos and threes, against each other. It was round-robinish, and it worked to the delight of the audience.

I had been watching for signs from The Legend. Now some danger signals were making themselves felt and heard. She seemed to be winding down slowly, like a clock that has become tired in the mainspring. What the enervating process was I could not be sure. My best guess was we were nearing the end of the first thirteen. Ahead lay the uncertainty of new people to work with and relate to. The eight shows Jewison superintended had begun promisingly, but in spite of good reviews, the show was a poor second in the ratings to "Bonanza." Judy knew it and so did her managers, and so did CBS. While Glenn Ford was still very much in the picture, he had started a film, and his leisure time was now severely limited. Since Judy regarded Jewison as a transient, she had fallen back on Gary Smith as her copilot on the Dawn Patrol. As she had expressed no great love for him, his company must have been unsatisfactory at best.

I had been watching the metamorphosis take place, slowly, since that day in the trailer when she had exulted over the New York reviews. There was nothing I could do to help the situation except to be available as a sounding board if and when she needed me. Sure enough, that weekend she called and invited Snow White and myself over for Sunday dinner. Other people were arriving when we got to her house, among them Jewison and Gary Smith. After dinner we watched that week's air show, which was, unfortunately, the one I have previously mentioned as being below standard, guest-wise, as far as Garland was concerned.

When it was over, everyone made an attempt to rationalize why that particular show did not work, but their efforts were pointless. Judy had disliked it from the beginning, and no amount of "copping out" would suffice. Glenn Ford, who had been Judy's host at dinner, had an early-morning studio call. He and most of the other guests departed early. Little Joey and Lorna said good night as soon as their mother's show was finished, and Snow White and I found ourselves alone with Judy. We made ready to leave, and Judy said she wanted a few words with me. I was afraid she would unburden herself in front of Snow White, thereby giving my wife more ammunition to fire at me; and since I already had the wagons in a circle, warding off her barbed comments about the show, I wisely suggested we put off talking until the next day, pleading fatigue. Judy was strangely docile that evening. She nodded her head quietly, thanked us for coming and said good night.

She did not come to work at all on Monday, but Tuesday she put in an appearance at my office, which was unusual. She had not entered that room more than three or four times since the show had begun. "Take me to lunch," she ordered.

We went to the Polo Lounge of the Beverly Hills Hotel.

She had no appetite. She ordered a large vodka on the rocks. As the waiter walked away, she said, directly, "It's not working, is it? It will never work!"

I tried to play it cute. "That's what they told Robert Fulton."

"No jokes today," she snapped. "What are you always saying? 'Straight life?' That's the way you better talk now!"

I had slept badly the night before. I was in a low-tolerance mood.

"What do you want from me, Judy? What can I say that you don't already know? Or think you know?"

"I *know* I know. My show's down the toilet. Oh, we can go right on taping, but it isn't going to get any better."

I grunted. "Hope springs eternal." Before she could object to the banality, I continued. "Look, nobody's dumb enough to count you out. Ever. And that includes you yourself. We've been coasting these last few shows, sure. I've been as guilty of it as anyone else. There's been a feeling of, I don't know, call it impermanence around the old corral. That's not your fault or mine. It's just how it is. But what the hell, why not look on the bright side? Two more shows and you can take a rest while CBS finds you a nice new creative team to make you look brilliant."

She looked forlorn. "And how the hell can I be sure the new geniuses will be any better than the old ones?"

"Oh, well, if you're looking for a sure thing, then stop singing altogether and dump all your money into A T and T."

The waiter brought her drink and my shrimp cocktail. She took a good, strong belt, grimaced and said, "Christ, you're a real comfort to me in my old age."

"I thought you said 'no jokes'?"

Gloomily, she replied, "I'm not joking. I feel a hundred and ten today!"

"Well, Zelda, you're not acting a hundred and ten."

"Zelda?" she laughed, nearly choking on her drink. "When did I graduate to 'Zelda'?"

"I think," I said, forging ahead, "that we've made progress during these last six shows. I know you were depressed last night after seeing the air show, but that was just bad luck. It was a weak show, and you knew it all along. You shouldn't have even watched it, in my opinion. But OK, you did. Now it's over. Let me ask you something. Haven't you ever been in a lousy movie?"

"Are you kidding? Too many!"

"Well, I don't agree, but for the moment, kick this thought around. You make a bad picture, it comes out, the reviews stink, the public stays away in droves, and you're dog meat until your next one's released. How many movies can you make in a year? Three if you break your back? Right! So the people have to wait months to see if you and your next picture are any better than this turkey they just saw and hated. On the other hand, last Sunday night's show is gone with the wind, and this coming Sunday night's epic is the June Allyson, Steve Lawrence show, which you loved. Or have you changed your mind about that one?"

"No," she admitted, "that was a damned good show."

"Okay. So at ten o'clock Sunday night you're an instant heroine all over again."

She smiled. "I know you're trying to cheer me up . . ."

"Don't I always?"

"—but I can't shake this feeling of failure. I just can't."

"Baby," I said gently, "you've never been able to shake it.

I don't think you know how good you are! Did I ever tell you about Fred Astaire?"

She looked surprised. "What's he got to do with this?"

"Simply this: he's my idol, my favorite singer, did you know that? I think he reads a lyric better than anyone I ever heard," quickly adding, "except you, Sarah Bernhardt, except you. Anyway, I made an album a few years ago called 'Mel Tormé Sings Fred Astaire,' and frankly, just for the sheer kick of talking to The King, I got his telephone number and called him, on the pretext of asking his advice about what tunes to pick, et cetera. I couldn't believe that conversation. He continually ran himself down, said he didn't think he could sing at all and was genuinely astounded that I would even consider doing an LP around him and the songs he introduced in his movies. He honestly does not know how great he is. And neither do you." I was wound up, and if I was ever going to get a few things off my chest, this was the propitious time.

"Part of what's wrong, Jude, *is* you. On some of the shows you've done, you've been hanging in there, rehearsing, encouraging your cast and your guests, just beautiful. But on many others, and last Sunday night's is a prime example, you've lost interest early. You've waltzed your way through the taping. And the result has been the same every time." I made a circle of my thumb and forefinger and held it up. "Lousy," I said.

Her jaw muscles clenched. "How many of these little talks have we had?"

"Too many. I don't like playing football coach, but sometimes you seem to crave it."

She looked into her drink. "You really feel that most of what's wrong is my fault?"

"Don't do that, lady. Don't paraphrase me. I said *some* of it is. I haven't weighed it on a scale. But I told you before, don't look back. How about the fifteen shows ahead of us? Why don't we make a tremendous effort to do the greatest shows anyone's ever seen?"

She didn't answer me directly. She drained her glass, called to the waiter for a refill, and said, "So when are you going to record 'Mel Tormé Sings Judy Garland'?"

That luncheon meeting seemed to act as a stimulant. On the very next show, she was at peak form, singing "Moon River" against a rather fetching harmonica obbligato I had contrived and joining guest Vic Damone in excerpts from *Porgy and Bess.* Since Vic probably has the finest vocal instrument of any pop crooner-singer in the business, Judy was on her mettle to match him. Together they made the Gershwin classics something to hear. For a closer, she belted out "Rock-a-bye Your Baby with a Dixie Melody" and the regulars clapped their hands off.

The thirteenth and final show in the first cycle found her invigorated and involved mainly because we had lured Peggy Lee onto the program to make one of her rare television appearances. Once again, Garland's spirit of competitiveness was aroused, and once again, she rose to the occasion and more than held her own opposite the magnificent Peg. For comedy, there was Jack Carter, and for "Tea," Carl Reiner. It was a good show, particularly to end the first cycle with, and Judy invited everyone into the trailer afterward for a drink.

Sultan and Worth dropped in to say good-by to her. They had barely gotten to know her during the eight shows they had written, and since they had other projects going around town, they had been AWOL for much of the final two or three shows. Jewison kissed her good-by, spouting words of love, wisdom and advice. I thought I noticed a marked look of relief on his face.

When everyone had cleared out except her agents, Glenn and myself, she sighed and said, "Well, we made it through the first thirteen. Nobody thought we would, but we did! I wonder how the great Mr. Aubrey likes them apples?"

We spoke of the future shows fleetingly. Judy was in a "Que sera, sera" frame of mind, and for now, that wasn't bad. Ahead lay a few weeks of rest while staff number three pulled itself together. Then we would have at it all over again. Since tonight's show had *felt* triumphant, with Glenn in the audience, smiling at her and applauding harder than anyone else, Garland was in a euphoric mood, exuding charm and graciousness, the epitome of ladylike femininity.

Not long after, we said our good nights, accompanied by hugs and kisses and promises to get together in the next week or so for a social evening. I got into the elevator and punched "One." As I walked down the long corridor toward the artists' exit, I passed the guard desk. On the wall behind him was a large calendar. It was Friday, November 8, 1963. It had taken over five months to get thirteen shows on tape.

Chapter 7

Two Fridays later, I awoke early and looked out the bedroom window. The clouds were playing tag with the sun, and there was a decided chill in the air. Winter's coming, I thought idly as I dressed for breakfast. Well, at least this kind of weather breaks the monotony of one semi-tropical day after another, and the smog factor is at a minimum. Since I had first come out to California, the most interesting season of all had seemed to me to be late fall and winter, with genuine fog rolling in off the Pacific and rain freshening the air and glistening on the foliage.

Snow White made breakfast for me. As I ate she asked, "What's happening today? Where are you going?"

"Don't you remember? I record that stuff I wrote for KSFO today."

"Oh, the San Francisco thing. Will you be home for dinner?"

"I think so. We've got about forty-nine separate pieces of music to do, but, with luck, we ought to finish up late this afternoon."

I looked out the breakfast-room windows at the sky and said, "Hmmm. Wonder if it's going to rain. It's tough to find a parking space around United Recorders. Thought I'd take the bike, but I don't want to ride it in the rain."

"They said on TV last night there was only a twenty percent chance of rain today."

"Really? Should be all right then, huh?"

"Should be."

Mundane little scenes like the foregoing were the least dangerous form of communication between my wife and myself. Since the Garland show had gone on this current hiatus, Snow White and I had carefully skirted the danger zones by mutual agreement and had been making an effort to walk the well-defined path of commonplace conversation. I was not deceiving myself. Nothing was going to be miraculously solved by adopting this behavior pattern, but at least it made for peace in the house.

I got into a turtleneck and a black leather-and-wool jacket and, insulated against the cold, made my way on motorcycle toward Hollywood. With the exception of having sung the title song for a picture called *Sunday in New York* at Metro a week before, I had done very little during the layoff. I was looking forward to cutting the KSFO spots, many of which I had written over a period of the last four weeks.

I parked my bike conveniently near the recording studio, which was located on Sunset Boulevard near Columbia Pictures. As I turned the key in the fork lock, I looked at my watch. It was ten fifty. The session was due to begin at eleven. Next door to United was Hollywood Film Enterprises, a lab that was processing some film of mine. I walked in, went to the counter and saw Jim Turner, with whom I usually dealt.

"Hi, James," I said. "My film ready?"

He looked a bit strange. "Did you hear what happened?" he asked.

"No, what?"

"They shot the President."

"Aw, come on Jim, let me have my film and get out of here. I've got forty-five people waiting for me next door and——"

"I'm not kidding. They just shot Kennedy. In Dallas."

I looked around the office. The employees stood rooted in their tracks, looking like figures in a wax museum. Jim said, "Isn't it terrible? What is this country coming to?"

I shook my head. "I don't know, Jim. I just don't know. How bad is it? Is he——"

"Dead? No, they've rushed him to a hospital. Nobody seemed to know how serious the wound is."

Dazed by the news, I walked out of the place without waiting for my film. When I entered United Recorders next door, all the musicians were in the foyer, listening to the reports on the radio. Marty Paich, who had orchestrated my music on this date, walked up to me.

"Do you believe it, man?" he asked querulously. "Do you believe a nitwit who would shoot Kennedy?" He shook his head disgustedly. "Wow! What the hell is this country coming to?"

One of the KSFO execs who had flown down for the day now walked over, said hello and asked, "Do you think we should cancel the session? I mean, who's going to feel like singing and playing?"

"No one, that's for sure," I replied. "It's too bad you've come all the way from up north for nothing. What about the singers? How do they feel about it?"

"They're in the studio, rehearsing. They don't know about the shooting yet."

"I better tell them," I said, my shoulders sagging.

I walked into the studio to find a totally different atmosphere. Jud Conlon was putting the chorus through its paces, joyously singing my little bits and pieces. He saw me, smiled, waved his arms to cut off the singing and said, "Hey, baby, I like these little things you've written. They're fun to sing."

The singers, most of whom I had worked with before, waved and called hello. Bernie Parke, who had been one of my original Mel-Tones, said, "What's the matter, Melvie? You look like you've lost your best friend."

I grimaced. "Listen, everyone. Some piece of walking garbage just shot President Kennedy in Dallas."

There were instant "ohs" and "good Gods" from the group. Jud shook his head and said "Lord, what's this country coming to?"

I gathered all the musicians and singers together in the studio and asked for a vote regarding going ahead with the session or canceling it. The general consensus was that we would accomplish nothing by postponing the date. The news was bad, and if we elected to scrub the recording, we would only all go home or to a bar and drink and brood. At least, if we went ahead with the "promos," it would keep us occupied and take our minds off the tragedy.

We started to rehearse the first piece of music. Bill Putnam, United's owner and chief recording engineer, tapped on the glass of the booth and held up the phone. I excused myself and went inside to answer it. It was Snow White.

"Did you hear about the President?"

"Yeah, I heard. Any more news? How is he?"

"He just died, Mel. They announced it a minute ago on television."

"Sweet Jesus!" I hung up, went out into the studio and told the others. Again I polled them, but they still voted to go ahead. I guess they knew we would all weep for our dead leader throughout the entire weekend, not to mention the rest of our lives. Time enough this evening to talk about it with family and friends, to sift through the incredible events of the day, to watch television nonstop as the various commentators made their observations on the assassination and its effect on our lives and the course of history. Around twelve thirty, I suggested we break for lunch. No one was hungry, or so it appeared. "Let's keep going, get it done," was the general attitude. Midafternoon, and a sudden thought struck me. Oh, my God! Judy! I'll bet she's heartbroken, remembering JFK's phone call and telegram.

Late in the day, we finished the recording, quietly said our good-bys and left the studio. I stepped out onto Sunset Boulevard into a world seemingly gone mad. Sirens were sounding from every direction, why I could not tell. It sounded like London during the Blitz. I rode the cycle home slowly and carefully. I was tired and cold, and I knew the shivering I was experiencing was only partly the chill wind that knifed through my jacket. As I headed west on Sunset I saw life around me going on as usual. People were chatting casually as they walked on the sidewalks. At a red light, a car with two couples in it pulled up alongside me, and the occupants were laughing and chattering animatedly.

Theater marquees were lit, traffic was proceeding normally, and outside of the wail of the sirens, vari-pitched, like so many out-of-tune banshees in the nights, it was hard to believe that a catastrophe of such mind-blowing enormity had taken place earlier in the day. The Strip had just begun to deteriorate into Hippie Heaven, and as I glided past its wild-haired habituées with their leather-thong sandals, ponchos and wide-brimmed Apache Indian sombreros, as I watched, even at this early hour, a queue beginning to form outside Whiskey A Go Go, I thought again of the phrase I had heard repeated so often that day: what is this poor, sick, confused, alienated country of mine coming to?

When I got home I tried calling Judy. She was not in, I was informed. When would she return? They did not know.

All standard programing had stopped, the day's events preempting everything. As I lay in bed, red-eyed, glued to the TV set, the chronology of disaster unfolded over and over again. The capture of Oswald in a moviehouse, the fatal shooting of Officer Tippett, the breakneck dash to Parkland Hospital in an attempt to save a life that Jackie Kennedy knew had already been snuffed out, as she cradled the shattered head of her husband in the back seat of the black limousine.

I dozed off around two in the morning. Suddenly Snow White nudged me. "There's Judy," she said, as I came awake and focused my eyes on the screen. Television cameras observed Garland leaving Pat Kennedy Lawford's home. She looked terrible. Her eyes were dull, lifeless, her mouth drawn in a tight line, grim with grief. A newsman attempted to interview her. She waved him aside. Then another newscaster with whom she was acquainted blocked her way and gently prodded her for information. How is Mrs. Lawford

taking it? Did you know the President personally? How do
you feel about the assassination? She could only shake her
head over such inanity.

"It's"—she struggled for words—"it's too much, it's—
just—*too much,*" she blurted out, and made her escape into
a waiting car.

I tried calling her early in the morning and again at noon.
She was incommunicado, taking no calls, answering no
questions. There was little incentive to get up, get dressed
and engage in normal activity that day. I stayed in bed,
peering at the TV set through bloodshot eyes as stories,
some of them beyond belief, rolled into the news centers and
were related to the viewing public.

One rumor had it that a grade-school classroom in Dallas,
upon hearing of the assassination, had burst into cheers!
Night life throughout the country had flourished the previous evening as the President's corpse lay in its coffin on
board *Air Force One* heading for Washington. During several man-in-the-street interviews conducted throughout the
nation, more than one great sidewalk humanitarian was
quoted as saying, "Well, let's face it! He asked for it, didn't
he? I mean, a lot of people I know think he got what he
deserved." One had to listen to these reports, shake one's
head as if recovering from a Joe Louis right cross, and go
on to the next bit of information.

Next day, Sunday, unkempt, unshaven, I woke up early,
had a bite of breakfast in my robe and slippers and went
back to bed. I turned on the TV for company and tried to
read, but it was no use. I kept going over the same para-
graph again and again, not really knowing what I had read.
Then something so unbelievable happened that, even though
I saw it with my own eyes, my mind refused to accept it.

Jack Ruby, in front of millions of television viewers, pulled a snub-nosed .38 and shot Lee Harvey Oswald as he was being moved to other quarters by members of the Dallas police department. The tape of the event was run repeatedly in the next few hours, and every time I saw it, it seemed to be a scene from "Naked City" or "Dragnet." As Judy had so aptly put it, it was just too much. The brain is receptive to a certain amount of incredulity, but the fantastic happenings of the last thirty-six hours, topped by this latest absurdity, were simply beyond the boundaries of credibility. Someone called that evening, I forget who, and asked, "What do you think of Oswald getting killed like that?"

Wearily, I said, "It's all a 'B' picture. It's comic-strip stuff. If it were made into a movie nobody would believe it." Indeed, at that moment, I recalled a Sinatra film called *Suddenly,* in which he played a kind of Oswald character who tries to murder the President. Well, I thought, they can burn *that* negative. No one's ever going to run that thing again. How wrong I was! I am astounded and ashamed to say that the film has played many times on TV throughout the country since Kennedy's death.

Through the medium of television my family mourned, along with the rest of the nation, on Monday, as the draped coffin, followed by the riderless horse and accompanied by the muffled tattoo of drums made its way slowly down Pennsylvania Avenue toward the President's final resting place, Arlington Cemetery.

The next day we were to resume production of the show with the third cast of characters. Halfheartedly, I wandered into the office and shook hands with the team of writers signed to replace Sultan and Worth, two Canadians named Peppiatt and Aylesworth. Jewison's replacement was Bill

Colleran, a veteran television producer, and husband of actress Lee Remick. It was an unfortunate day to make new acquaintances and start working again. We were all drained from the events of the last four days, and no one could muster much enthusiasm. We had not heard from Judy, and speculation was rife that she would not be in that day or perhaps even all week, which would effect a cancelation of Friday's taping.

However, as I sat in my office, late in the morning, the phone rang and to my surprise it was Garland calling me from the trailer. She asked me to come to her right away, and when I suggested bringing the writers and Colleran along, she said no, just come alone.

I tried, when she greeted me, to express my concern over her feelings in connection with the President's death. She refused to discuss it. Instead she said, "I want to scrap this week's show."

I wasn't surprised. "You mean, you want to wait a week or so to go back to work, huh? Well, I can't blame——"

"I mean I want to do a show this week. No guests, no sets, just the orchestra and me. That's why I asked you to come down here. I want to discuss what I have in mind with you alone. And I want you to tell me, honestly, what you think of my idea. All right?"

"Of course."

She looked tired as she gazed out the window of her trailer into the corridor. If she is an insomniac under normal circumstances, I thought, how much sleep can she have had over the last seventy-two hours? Damn little, I was certain.

"I want to do," she began, "a concert of great American songs. I think it's important right now, maybe more important than ever to have a kind of—reaffirmation of faith in our country and what it stands for. I don't intend to make this a tribute to Jack Kennedy. Nothing will be said, very little talk, if any, just an hour concert of songs like 'Home on the Range,' 'America the Beautiful,' 'Keep the Home Fires Burning'—great songs."

I was genuinely moved by the idea and I told her so. Her face lit up. "Oh, I'm so glad. I'm *so* glad," she cried. "Would you please go upstairs and sell Bill Colleran on it?"

I promised I would. I believed that, done tastefully, very low-key, sparsely produced, it could be one of the most important hours in television history.

I called Colleran from my office and told him I had something to discuss. He asked me to come right in. Bill Colleran was undoubtedly the gentlest of the three executive producers with whom I had been associated. Of medium height, he bore a superficial resemblance to the late actor Myron McCormick, with thinning hair, an Everyman countenance, clothing in conservative taste—either business suits or tweedy sports jackets and slacks. He was a pipe smoker, which surprised no one, and he gave an overall impression of total affability. These days, he was looking a bit fragile. He had only recently escaped death in a serious auto accident. In addition, I had been told his marriage to Lee Remick was on shaky ground, a reconciliation having been effected just recently after a separation of some length. I wondered what effect his Garland duties would have on the eventual outcome of his marital status. Just as quickly, I decided it was none of my business.

I outlined Judy's idea.

"Marvelous, marvelous," he said, running the words together, as he had a habit of doing. "A great idea."

"Good, Bill. I'm glad you like it. Now I guess you have to pick up the ball and run with it."

He stood up, took the pipe out of his mouth, pointed the stem northward and said, "Right into Aubrey's office."

Twenty minutes later, he returned, looking dejected.

"Aubrey says no," he said, disappointment plainly written on his features.

"But why, Bill? It's such a valid idea, especially right now."

"Well, he pointed out that the whole country has been in mourning for the past four days. Now he wants to get back to normal programing."

"No chance he'll change his mind?"

"No, none. He's firm about it. He wants us to do the show originally scheduled."

"Gee, that's too bad. He may be right, who knows? It's just that this is the first time Judy has pushed hard for a specific conception on any show. I hate like hell to see her shot down in flames."

"*You* hate it? This is my first show, remember? I'm supposed to be daddy, taking care of his little girl. Now I've got to go tell her there is no Santa Claus."

"Look, would I be out of line if I offered to——"

"Thanks, Mel, but it's my place to break the news. God, she's going to be unhappy about this."

That turned out to be the understatement of the year. Garland was livid. Then she graduated to cold fury. From that day on, her dislike of Aubrey turned to real hatred, and she railed against him at every opportunity. She accepted his edict and went ahead with the first show in the new cycle, but she nursed her enmity like a newborn babe and pledged a vendetta at some future time.

That first show gave the new staff a rough idea of Life With The Legend. She barely rehearsed that week, clearly apathetic. We opened with a football medley, featuring Judy and a number of kids. First it was in, then it was out, then in again. Judy exhibited equal amounts of disinterest and indecision. Her songs and talk with guests Bobby Darin and Bob Newhart were adequate, nothing more. Peter Gennaro was the new choreographer, and he contributed some bright moments by performing with the dancers, but generally, it was an inauspicious third beginning.

I was enjoying my new association with Peppiatt and Aylesworth, a pair of totally zany, lovable characters. In addition, their writing talents were strictly top drawer. If anyone can make this show work, I thought, it's these two daffy guys. They were also fellow movie nuts, with a real penchant for English war films. Peppiatt, a big bear of a man with spaced teeth and an infectious smile, never called me by name. Instead, as was his right, as self-appointed "Captain," he referred to me as "Number One" (an English naval term applied to the first officer of a ship). His partner, cherub-faced, sandy-haired John Aylesworth, a puppy-dog of a guy who even on the hottest days of the year always looked as if he had just come from an open-air ice-skating rink in snowbound Wisconsin, was never known as anything other than "Binky." Whenever I walked into my office in the morning, the Captain would stick his huge head in the door and say (in a refined English accent, of course): "Oh, hello, Number One. How's refitting coming along?"

"Good-o, sir," I would reply in kind. "I've only just returned from 'stores' and they've promised we'll be operational in a fortnight."

"Capital! Can't wait to get cracking. These bloody Hun wolfpacks are playing hell with our convoys."

"Too true."

"Yes," he would reply, rubbing the bowl of a pipe against his nose. "Well, there it is, i'nt it? Keep after them, Number One. The rotten sods will lay about on their backsides until tea unless they've got the wind up. That's where you come in, right?"

"Right, sir. They're a good lot, though. Mustn't grumble."

He would then give me a peremptory salute, palm forward, British-style (which, I naturally, would return), and disappear. There were days when the above was virtually the only conversation that passed between us. Admittedly, it was a silly game, yet oddly necessary to preserve sanity in the delicate atmosphere of this new regime.

The following Monday, Colleran wandered into my office and told me Judy had requested that I participate in the next show, which was to be our Christmas offering. Since Jack Jones had already been signed as the guest star, I was requested to consider this a token appearance, not one of my regular guest shots, and my remuneration was suggested accordingly. My first reaction was to decline, politely. The money mentioned was a joke, if not an insult, and with Jack carrying the major load of male singing chores, there certainly would not be much left for me.

I told Colleran I would rather not. Gary Smith went to work on me. Judy had asked him to ask me, and so forth. Then she called me personally.

"Mel, I understand you don't want to be on the Christmas show."

"No, that's not quite accurate. I said I would *rather* not be on it."

"Any special reason?"

"Well, yes, frankly. Money, for one. And please don't misunderstand, Jack Jones for another. He's the guest this week, and he deserves the most guest time. That makes me low man on the pole, and I don't dig being in that position."

"Did you know all my kids are going to be on this one?"

"Yes, Colleran told me."

"I'd like to make it a real family show, in a living room set. I thought I could sing your 'Christmas Song,' with you playing it for me, and what about you and Jack doing a carol together, a capella? I know that would be great!"

She sounded enthusiastic, and that was not to be sneezed at.

"Hey," I laughed, "you're doing my job for me. First it's 'Get Happy' with Streisand, now it's Jones and Tormé, snappy patter and Christmas carols a specialty."

"I'd consider it a personal favor if you'd do it," she cooed. I sighed. Money isn't everything, I thought. "Okay, Sadie, you got yourself a pigeon."

That was Monday.

Tuesday, all went relatively well. Judy showed up mid-afternoon to discuss songs for her children on the show. I remember she was particularly witty that day, laughing with Peppiatt and Aylesworth, chatting volubly with Bill Colleran and being especially courteous and friendly toward Gary, which was becoming more and more unusual. When she left for home at five that afternoon someone quipped, "Hell, we ought to book her kids on every show for the remainder of the series, if it makes her this happy!"

The Dawn Patrol finally caught up to me. That very night. Or rather, early Wednesday morning. One minute all

was quiet and peaceful. The next the phone by my bed
jangled off the hook, and without thinking, I groped for it
in the dark.

"Hullo," I mumbled.

"Mel? Mel?" It was Judy. She sounded terror-stricken.

"Judy? What's wrong?"

"Oh, God, Mel, come quick. Please! I need you. I'm in
trouble!"

Now I was wide awake. I turned on the bedside light as
Snow White asked who it was. I put my finger to my lips.

"What is it, Jude? What's the matter? What kind of———"

"I can't talk now. Not here."

"Where are you?"

"At home."

"Well, then, why can't you———"

"Please come over. Right away. Get me out of here."

I looked at the clock on the nightstand. "It's four thirty
in the morning, Judy. You should be sleeping. We've got a
runthrough today with Liza and Joey and———"

"Gonna be no runthrough. Gonna be no show unless you
come get me. RIGHT AWAY!" she shouted. I did not answer directly. She was breathing heavily on the other end
of the line.

"She drunk?" asked Snow White.

"Don't know," I answered, covering the phone. "Sounds
like she might be."

"Well, HOW ABOUT IT?" Judy roared in my ear. "Are
you coming or not?"

"I think I better get over there," I whispered to my wife.
To Judy I said, "All right. Take it easy. I'll be there as soon
as I can."

"Mel," she said quietly.

"Yes?"

"HURRY, GODDAMIT!"

I put on my clothes in the dark, told Snow White to go back to sleep and headed for the Garland residence.

When I arrived, light was spilling through the partially open front door. I braked the Corvette to a stop, got out and looked around tentatively. From the way Judy had carried on, I half-expected to see someone emerge from the house, covered in blood, a smoking revolver in his hand. Nothing seemed amiss, as far as I could tell.

I walked inside to find Judy, fully dressed, looking for something in a desk. She handed me a tote bag she was holding with a terse, "Take this," and continued looking through the drawers. "Can't leave without my books. Gotta take my books with me," she babbled, nearly incoherent. She pushed past me to look in another area, and I got a whiff of her. Whoever propagated the myth regarding vodka and its undetectability on the human breath should have his own breath examined.

After a few moments, she found what she had been looking for: three looseleaf address books in various colors of vinyl. "Th'rall th'same," she explained. "But can't leave 'em here. Can't. Sid might get 'em. Gotta take 'em with me." She dumped them into the tote bag and said, "C'mon, let's go."

"Go? Where?"

"Where d'ya think, stupid? Your house."

She got into the car while I stood there for a moment, undecided. It would mean waking Snow White again, plus Tracy, plus the maid, probably. At five thirty in the December morning, while it was still dark out. The trouble was there did not seem to be any alternatives.

As we were heading east on Sunset Boulevard, she rambled on, blurry-tongued, barely understandable. "My sister Sue—she's dead. Called me and asked for help—I tried—got my own troubles—did you know my sister?—No, y'never met her—we were never very close, but I loved 'er —loved my sister a lot—loved both my sisters—did you ever meet my sisters?"

I mentioned that I had known "Jimmy," the younger of her two sisters, when she had dated my songwriting partner, Bob Wells. Garland took no notice.

"We were good, you know that? The Gumm sisters. We had fun singing together. Long time ago," she said, forlornly. "*Long* time ago. Did you know my dad was a good singer? And writer? He wrote 'I Will Come Back,' did you know that? No, you didn't. You're so wrapped up in your own damn world, you never took time to find out about mine."

I answered this last with silence, keeping my eyes on the road, which, even at this early hour, was beginning to get busy with traffic.

She remained quiet for a minute. Then she said, "I'm sorry."

"It's all right."

"Oh, Christ, don't pull that nobler-than-thou shit on me. I said I was sorry, and I am sorry. Now, for God's sake, at least be gracious about it."

"Give me a minute, and I'll think of something clever to say."

"You usually do. That's your problem. You're so god-damned clever. Your singing is clever, your writing is clever, your *ass* is clever. Clever, clever, clever, that's you."

"Yeah, well, that's why you hired me, isn't it? To cleverly write your clever little show and make you look clever?"

"I don't have to take this. Stop the car."

I screeched to a halt on a curve in Westwood. A few cars whizzed by, drivers peering at me to see if I was in trouble.

"All right, clever man, take me home."

"A pleasure."

I started to make an illegal U-turn, but she grabbed the wheel and tugged at it violently. "Not my home, schmuck, yours."

We drove the rest of the way to my house in silence, her head hung between her shoulders, eyes staring straight ahead through grotesquely large, smoke-colored sunglasses.

As cars passed me in both directions, I looked at them and thought, "Hey, folks, be happy on your way to work this morning, to your normal, everyday jobs that you believe to be glamourless and unexciting. Because to my immediate right sits one of the world's great symbols of glamour and excitement, and, no fooling, you ain't missing a thing!"

When we arrived at my house, I prevailed upon Snow White to take care of Judy, who was now fading fast. My wife took her into our bedroom, undressed her and prepared to help her bathe, while I repaired to the guest bedroom to try and sleep a few more hours before heading for the office.

"Try to get her to sleep," I whispered. "I don't think she's been to bed yet at all, and we have an important day ahead of us."

I settled into the guest bed and had just dozed off when Snow White came into the room and exclaimed, "God, you ought to see her back! It's covered with marks—I guess you'd call them welts, as if someone has been beating her!"

There was no sense trying to figure out how or why the

marks had gotten there, and I cautioned her not to ask Judy about them.

"Just get her into our bed and off to sleep."

She agreed and went back to the master bedroom.

Once again, I dropped off. The house was quiet. Little Tracy had slept through Judy's arrival, and I was dreaming pleasant dreams when I heard a commotion in the hallway. I opened my tired eyes just as my wife came bursting into the room.

"Oh, my God, Mel," she cried excitedly. "She just swallowed about *thirty* pills! I think she's trying to kill herself."

I leaped out of bed and ran to our bedroom. Judy lay in my bed, out like a light. Her breathing seemed shallow, and her color was not good.

"We've got to get a doctor, quick!" I said.

I called a physician I knew. "She *what?*" he asked.

"She just popped a whole handful of pills in her mouth. Please, you have to come over. Right away. I'm afraid she's going to die."

Calmly, he replied, "Forget it. I wouldn't touch her with a ten-foot pole. Did you know," he added casually, "I used to be her doctor a few years ago?"

"Listen, you son of a bitch, get your ass over here. Now! I have a woman who may be dying, and you're telling me the story of your life!"

He laughed. "Relax, relax! What color were the pills she took?"

I asked Snow White, who told me, and I relayed the information on to him.

"Don't worry about it. She eats those pills like you eat Cracker Jacks. She'll be all right. Just let her sleep them off."

"Are you sure?"

"At seven fifteen in the morning I'm not sure of anything."

"Well, then——"

"I'm only kidding. Sure I'm sure. She'll be fine." And, with a touch of sarcasm, "She always is."

I gave up the idea of sleep. Fuzzy-headed, I ate breakfast in a stupor. Snow White was also up for the day. As she sat at the breakfast table, resting her head on her arm, I voiced my concern.

"The good doctor says she'll be okay, so I don't think we have any worries on that score. I don't see how doing a show this week is possible, though. We're supposed to have run-through today at one o'clock. You know, her kids are on this one. That makes the show tricky unless we get a good rehearsal this afternoon. I just don't think we can go ahead with it."

"Why worry about it? Why don't you just dump it in—whatizname—the producer's lap?"

"Colleran? Oh, God, what am I going to tell him?"

"The truth, of course."

"Yeah. Yeah, I guess that's all I can do."

But when I got to the office, I withheld the information. I have never believed in miracles, yet I kept hoping for one, although the odds were a hundred to one against such a phenomenon occurring. Judy had, I told myself, pulled other marginal shows out of the fire. Maybe, this time, she could once again.

Was I doing a disservice to the people with whom I worked? Didn't they have a right to know what was happening? I looked at the clock on my desk. Nine fifteen. Plenty of time to be the spreader of bad tidings. I decided to hang fire and wait for that miracle.

Colleran came in about fifteen minutes later, greeted me cheerily and commented on my look of fatigue. I told him I had not slept well the previous night, which was true enough. As he walked into the main office for morning coffee, I was sorely tempted to tell him what had happened, to get it off my chest and let him carry the load. I kept silent—why, I don't know.

At ten after ten, my phone rang. It was Snow White.

"She's up!"

"Oh, fine."

"She's yelling her head off for Glenn Ford. What'll I do?"

"I don't know. I'll see if I can find him. Jesus, didn't she sleep at all?"

"About an hour and forty-five minutes altogether."

"There goes the Christmas show," I groaned.

I walked into Colleran's office, and as casually as possible, I asked for Glenn Ford's number. I quickly added he had asked me to find something in particular in the way of a Christmas gift for Judy, and I wanted to discuss it with him. "The Judy Garland Show" was making a proficient liar out of me.

I called Glenn's house. His mother answered. She sounded sweet-little-old-lady-mom's-apple-pie-ish.

"Glenn's working today, Mr. Tormé. On a boat, off Santa Monica. He'll be shooting until late this evening. Is anything wrong?"

"Uh—no, no. We've—uh—we've got a very good show going this week, and Judy—Miss Garland—was hoping maybe he could come to the runthrough—today—" It was weak, it was unconvincing. Even *I* didn't believe me.

"Well," she said, at a loss.

"Look, I'm sorry to have disturbed you, Mrs. Ford. If,

uh—if you hear from Glenn, please ask him to call me at my office. Or better still, have him call my house." I gave her the number. "Judy's having breakfast there with my wife." I thanked her and hung up. It was nearly ten twenty-five. At ten of eleven, Snow White called to tell me Glenn had gotten in touch with her, and she had outlined the situation to him. He had hung up abruptly.

Gary came in and asked if Judy had been contacted so far today. I told him no and continued to vamp till ready. I was fast running out of time and I knew I would have to make both Bill and Gary aware of the situation in a matter of minutes. Why I had waited so long as it is, I honestly could not rationalize to myself. Perhaps it was because, against almost insuperable odds, we had managed to get a show on the air every week up to now. I hated to see the record spoiled, particularly on this one, with Judy's kids participating.

At eleven thirty, Snow White called again, this time in a state of great agitation.

"Do you know what just happened? You're not going to believe it! It happened to me, and *I* still don't believe it!"

"What? What's the matter?"

She told me. Glenn had arrived at my house a few minutes before, unannounced and unexpected. Snow White had opened the door, recognized him and before she could even emit a sigh of relief, he had brushed her aside with his arm, looked around wild-eyed and yelled, "Where is she? Where are you keeping her?"

"Why, she's in our bed———"

He poked his index finger to within an inch of my wife's face and warned, "Don't you touch her! Don't you dare touch her! I'll take care of her. Where are her things? Where have you put them?"

"Now, look, Mr. Ford, you don't seem to understand. Judy woke us out of a sound sleep and we——"

"Never mind. Never mind that. Just take me to her."

Whereupon he made his way to the bedroom, lifted the exhausted Garland out of our bed and carried her bodily out to his car.

"Where are her things?" he cried accusingly at Snow White. "Have you kept any of her things?"

In answer, she ran inside, got Judy's tote bag, flung it at Glenn, said, "There! Now get the hell out of here!" and slammed the door.

Not having been present during this imbroglio, I can only repeat what was told to me. However, since Snow White related it while white hot with anger and insulted virtue, I have never for a moment doubted it happened, just the way she described it.

There was no question in my mind any longer about the status of the ball game. Called because of rain (or pills or booze or lack of sleep or what-have-you). I went in and unburdened my secret to Colleran and Smith. There was instant panic, followed by several choice oaths, followed by more panic. Colleran looked like a bomber pilot whose controls had just been shot away over Germany.

"What do we do now?" he said despairingly.

"Punt," I suggested, shrugging my shoulders.

"Could we repeat a show?" suggested Gary. "Maybe one of the early ones?"

"No," said Colleran. "I don't think CBS will buy that. We've only just begun the second thirteen. My God, this is only the second show, and we're in big trouble already!"

Gary could not suppress a smile. "Welcome to the club," he offered.

Colleran tried to call the Garland house. No answer. He called Glenn's home. No answer. He called her agents, Begelman and Fields, and gave them the word. It was a bright, sunshiny California day, but there were black thunderheads over Mudville. Mighty Casey had not slept, was unavailable for comment at the moment and that was that.

Bill said, "There's nothing to do, but tell the cast at one o'clock. We'll just have to cancel this one, pay everyone off and call it a draw. Aubrey's going to love this!" He looked miserable. He picked up the phone and called the front office. Aubrey was in a screening and would not be available until after lunch, around two o'clock. He hung up. "He'll find out about this soon enough. It's just as well he's out."

"Listen," said Gary, with a slight trace of anger, "why are we acting like it's the end of the world? We can't chain her to the trailer. Nobody can play watchdog twenty-four hours a day. We've all done our best! I've been in action on the Dawn Patrol since this show first got off the ground. Mel, you're now a charter member." I made a small bow.

"Anyway," Gary continues. "Enough is enough. I think we've done damn well to get as many shows on the air as we have. Now this one was just beyond our control. There's no sense in biting cyanide capsules over it. We just 'pass' this week. That's it."

"And what do we put on the air for the Christmas show?" asked Colleran.

"I honestly don't know," answered Gary bluntly. "And at this moment—this *very* moment—I just don't give a damn. In twenty minutes or so, I'll start to care like mad. But right now——"

Colleran smiled sadly. "Fellows, would you excuse me for a minute? I'd like to call my wife."

After lunch, which I hardly touched, I headed for the rehearsal hall.

I had hoped someone—anyone—had called to inform Liza and the kids about the canceled rehearsal, but when I opened the door to the hall, there they were, having been brought to CBS by chauffered limousine. They greeted me excitedly, thrilled at the prospect of appearing with momma, and jointly asked me what time she was arriving. Colleran heard their question and started over to talk to them. The rehearsal hall was noisy with chatter now, the singers, dancers and musicians all gabbing away. Jack Jones waved to me from the piano as he looked over the music.

Colleran herded the Garland brood into a corner.

"Listen, kids," he began, "we have a little prob——"

The rehearsal door swung open, and in walked Judy. Or, I should say, in *bounced* Judy. She was wearing her standard rehearsal costume, the now-familiar fisherman's hat, the soft white sandals, the slim slacks and gingham checked blouse. She flounced clear across the room, waving hello to the singers and dancers, pausing to kiss Jack Jones on the cheek, smiling, radiant, a decided spring in her step.

Her children ran to her, and she gathered them into her arms with cries of, "Hi, babies. Isn't this going to be fun? All of us together, singing on television, just like we do at home. Joey, did you learn your song?"

"Yes, Mom."

"Good. Well, let's get going."

I could only nod. I was speechless. I caught Colleran

looking at me strangely, as if to say, "What was all the shouting about? She's fine. She's beautiful, right as rain. Were you putting us on? She looks like she just slept for a week!" Gary Smith, on the other hand, nodded to me in understanding. He had been there before. We were soulmates.

As Judy went through her paces that afternoon, I could only look at her and marvel. How she had managed to return home, change clothes, do whatever she had to do to drag herself out of the sleepless abyss she must have been in and show up at Television City all within the course of an hour and a half was completely beyond me. Yet here she was, alert, alive, energetic, looking frighteningly normal. I thought of Johnny Bradford's description of her, "The Concrete Canary," and once again I realized how it fit her.

The Christmas show? Judy's favorite in the whole series. And one of mine as well. For in addition to the standard musical Christmas fare we offered up, Garland finally gave in and sang "Over the Rainbow" in the "Trunk" spot. She did it beautifully, in that soft, sweet little-girl voice I had admired in her early movies, the same voice I had heard on that first day in the rehearsal hall. As she finished singing and the applause swelled, I looked at her sitting on the edge of the stage, just as she had at the Palace, looking like a lost little waif, poignant and appealing, and I thought: In spite of everything, I am still a fan, Judy.

Chapter 8

"Forget about 'Born in a Trunk' this week. I have something special I want to do in that spot."

There was a grim determination about her decision to bypass our standard closing segment, and, at this first meeting of the week, she made her announcement, and looked around the room, clearly challenging anyone to question her right to do as she pleased.

All through that week, she kept her brainchild to herself, but, of course, total secrecy was impossible. Thursday night, the orchestra had to rehearse the song she had chosen, and though she did not sing it at that time, there was no mistaking what it was. Friday morning, and the name of the song was still not listed in the script. Everyone knew she was going to sing it, yet she had insisted it be deleted from the printed rundown, probably because she did not want CBS or Jim Aubrey to get wind of what she had planned until the actual taping took place.

All was sweetness and light now between Garland and Ethel Merman, her major guest that week. We had wrung everything we could out of "Be My Guest," and beginning with the Christmas show had decided to remove it from our format. Judy's stand-in introduced Ethel during runthrough, and that worthy lady, in her famous case-hardened manner, blared away with "Gee, But It's Good to Be Here," and the mandatory, "I Get a Kick Out of You." In trying to recapture the flavor of the earlier "Moon River" arrangement, I had written a similar harmonica obbligato against "Shenandoah," the well-known folk ballad. Once again the stand-in "sang-in" for the absent Garland, which did not worry me. Judy knew this song very well, and we had picked a comfortable key for her. She could sing it standing on her head.

Peter Gennaro went through his paces with the dancers, and in the booth, anxious eyes were beginning to look at clocks and watches. Now another guest, Shelley Berman, practiced his routine in front of the cameras. It was fast and funny, and the cast, crew and staff laughed, as much out of nerves as amusement. We were nearing dress-rehearsal time. No one had heard from our star. The show was running short, owing to Judy's demand regarding the "Trunk" department. Soon, the "Jewish Ladies From Fairfax Avenue" delegation would be ushered into the studio to watch the dry run of the show and Garland, even if she walked through the door right now, would be, for the most part, blissfully ignorant of what was going on. She had elected to remain away almost all week, only occasionally popping into the office to see if everything was copacetic, then flitting out again, not to be seen for the rest of the day. She was less prepared that week than she had been on almost any other show I could remember. When Colleran had called her home on Thursday, trying desperately to find her and induce her to come in for "blocking," he had been informed she was out, doing some Christmas shopping. She had not been present at any time during Thursday's activities.

Now, of course, as she arrived, minutes before we were to begin "Dress," there were audible sighs of relief, followed by expressions of concern regarding her ability to assimilate what was happening. We told her the show was several minutes short, with no forseeable way to lengthen it. "Put the 'Trunk' spot back in then," she said offhandedly. "It won't make any difference."

"Does that mean," began Colleran, "that you're not going to sing the other——"

"It means nothing of the sort," she snapped peevishly. "The show closes exactly as I planned."

She stumbled through dress rehearsal, barely knowing what she was doing. When it was over, as the nice little old ladies got up and walked out, I heard one of them exclaim, "Well, listen; she was good when she was a child, but personally, I liked Ethel Merman the best. *She,* already, is a star, and she didn't forget a single word, you noticed?"

Luckily, Judy did absorb enough during dress rehearsal to adequately hold her own throughout the taping. Finally, the "Trunk" spot came around. She rather listlessly made her way through a couple of songs, after which she made a very short little speech about the next song, saying it was something she very much wanted to sing, and she hoped the audience would understand. And then, as they waited expectantly, she sang "The Battle Hymn of the Republic."

It was a flawed performance, uneven musically, imperfect technically (at one point, her hand microphone went dead, and the audio staff at CBS spent the best part of three days "dubbing in" four or five words for the final "air" tape), but none of the foregoing mattered. Her timing was psychologically perfect. As she stood on the runway, eyes shining, head tilted upward "toward the heavens," singing:

> Mine eyes have seen the glory
> Of the coming of the Lord
> He is trampling out the vintage
> Where the grapes of wrath are stored . . .

I found myself crying. I was not alone. The big, burly cameraman next to me had tears running down his face. I looked around the studio. The people in the audience section were, almost uniformly, dabbing at their eyes with handkerchiefs and bits of Kleenex. As Judy continued to sing, making a slight retard at the end of the first chorus while the drums rolled into a crescendo opening the gate for the second chorus in a higher, brighter key, the tempo quickening slightly, I could almost hear the collective heartbeats in the place, and when that chorus was done, when I thought peak effectiveness had been attained, she planted her feet more firmly on the stage and sang yet a third chorus, one key higher, this time at a much slower, insistent tempo, each beat achieving a raw assertiveness of its own. When she eventually got to:

> "HIS—TRUTH—IS—
> MARRRR—CHING—ONNNNNNNNNN!"

she wrung out those final five words for every ounce of value they were worth. The emotion in the studio at that moment was purer than Ivory soap. Our dead president had not been in his grave three weeks. Though everything since his murder had taken on the appearance of business as usual, this was not the case. Reaction had set in after that nightmarish weekend, and the deep-down, gut-grinding hurt, the terrible sense of loss, was more prevalent than ever. Garland had touched a responsive chord in every man and woman in the audience that night.

Now they rose in a body and gave her the most genuine standing ovation I have ever witnessed. For this was acclaim that went beyond the mere love of an audience for a performer's talents. This was an appreciation of a human being. I remembered Schlatter saying, "We've got to humanize her, make the public identify with her." The public was having no trouble doing just that on the evening of December 13, 1963.

It would be unfair to question Judy's motive in choosing to sing "The Battle Hymn." Her genuine grief over Kennedy's untimely death cannot be doubted. I was well aware of her Pyrrhic victory over the imagined nemesis, Jim Aubrey. Whatever remained of any rapport between her and the heads of the network could have been dissolved that evening. And yet, I pondered, could they honestly object to her single-mindedness in paying tribute to our martyred head of state, especially when the spectators displayed such overwhelming approval? If Aubrey was angry, no one ever heard about it, and Judy, to her credit, refrained from gloating over the success she had enjoyed.

We had one more show to do before we took a breather during the Christmas holidays. Judy's adrenalin was coursing, possibly because, once again, Vic Damone was a guest, but more probably because the festive season was upon us and she would no doubt be going to several parties in the next few weeks squired by Glenn Ford.

Ken Murray, he of the ever-present cigar, appeared on that show, exhibiting home movies he had taken since his early days in Hollywood. They were nostalgic and delightful to see, including some footage he had shot of Judy when she was in her early teens. We decided to employ him on a regular basis, with his large fund of film replacing the "Tea for Two" department.

During that show, Judy issued invitations to the staff for a dinner party she was giving at Matteo's Restaurant in Westwood that evening. She was gayer than I had ever seen her that night, laughing, joking, giving out little presents, some of them innocuous gags, some very expensive. Late in the evening, when we were among the few patrons left in the place, she insisted on singing Christmas carols with me. Each successive carol was greeted with drunken cheers, and as we would finish one and begin another, Judy would grab me around the neck in a stranglehold and squeeze my face against hers. It was fun, and even Snow White seemed to get into the holiday spirit of things and enjoy herself. Around 2:00 A.M. we made our precarious way home. As we drove along Westwood Boulevard, my wife asked, "Hey, Mel, where was Glenn Ford tonight?" I had no answer to that one.

Since we were not expected to resume production until the first week in January, I flew to New York to do a concert at Carnegie Hall along with Count Basie and his band. It was a month to the day since the assassination had taken place. Though we played to a large house that night, we sensed the residue of grief that pervaded the atmosphere.

I had always wanted to sing at the famous Hall, but I was

sorry it had to be that night, so soon after JFK's passing.

I returned to Los Angeles in time for Christmas. I had mixed emotion about calling Judy. My adventure on the Dawn Patrol was still fresh in my mind. Why open a can of beans by calling and letting myself in, possibly, for a slew of sleep-destroyed nights before we went back to work in January? The only thing that kept nagging at me was Glenn Ford's absence at Matteo's. When I was tired of playing mental tug-of-war with myself, I gave in and called her.

"Judy?"

"Who's this?"

"Mel Tormé. Is that you, Sadie?"

"Hello, Mel. How are you?"

"Fine, just fine. How are you?"

"How did Carnegie Hall go?"

"Not bad. Good, really, considering everything."

"Everything?"

"Well, you know, only a month since the President was——"

"Oh, of course."

"Hey—uh—what's happening?"

"What do you mean?" She sounded listless, uninterested.

"I mean, what are you doing with yourself?"

"Oh, reading, spending time with the kids." She sounded as though she was in an introspective mood.

"Aren't you—getting out? Going to parties and all that?"

"No," she replied quietly.

"Listen, a truck usually has to hit me, but, uh—I sense all is not well between you and Glenn?"

"All is not well," she repeated to herself derisively. "All is bloody over and done with. *Alles ist kaput!* Finished. Period." She barked out the last word bitterly.

"Do I ask you what happened or do we just tactfully slide into another subject?"

"That's just it. I don't know what happened. One minute everything was fine, and the next we just weren't seeing each other anymore. Just like that. That quick."

"Judy, sometimes words are pretty lousy things, but if it means anything to you at all, I'm sorry."

"You're sweet. You really are. Of course it means something. It means a lot."

"Look, how about coming out to dinner with my wife and me? It's dumb to stay at home and brood, particularly this time of year."

"No thanks, Mel dear. In a crazy way, I'm kind of enjoying being by myself right now. What am I saying? I'm *not* alone. I've got Liza and Joey and Lorna, and you know something? They're really all I need. They're the only people who care for me. They don't give a damn how much money I've got or whether I'm working or starving or being applauded or sued. They just love me. So, I'm happy to just be with them. We sing together and watch TV and, uh"— she paused, thinking—"I'm—I'm all right, that's all. I'm just all right."

"Oh, well," I said, "lucky at kids, unlucky in love."

"Gee," she laughed, "did you just make that up? Wait a minute, let me get a pen and write it down. I want to remember it."

"Don't bother. I'll get my electric pencil, burn it into a block of wood and mail it to you."

"You're all heart, pal."

She stopped talking for a moment. "Mel?"

"Yeah, Judy?"

"It has been a little lonely. I don't want to see anyone

right now, but I do thank you for thinking of me. I need a lot of thinking about, especially now that Glenn and I . . ." she trailed off.

"I read you, Sadie. Loud and clear. Pick the phone up if you feel like talking."

"I will. Merry Christmas."

She hung up. A wave of relief swept over me, followed immediately by shame. What kind of phony creep are you becoming, I thought. You call her and invite her to dinner, hoping to God she'll say no. I tried to tell myself my reaction was natural, considering recent events, but myself was not buying. I kept seeing an imaginary finger shaking itself in my face. For shame! Still, the rationale was crystal clear in my mind. It would have been hypocritical not to admit Judy was a handful with a snootful. Experience had taught me she had very little resistance to adversity. It did not take much to push her over the edge toward the bottle or the pillbox or both; and though she had sounded perfectly sober on the phone, God only knew what the next few days would bring in the way of self-indulgence. I assuaged my guilty conscience by deciding to call her after Christmas and invite her out again, for New Year's Eve.

Fate, however, had other plans for me. On the twenty-eighth of December, as I was riding my bike down Sunset Boulevard toward Hollywood and a rendezvous with Snow White and Tracy in front of a theater, a car stopped suddenly and without warning directly in front of me, and in that split second, two thoughts crossed my mind: I wished I had taken Kennan Wynn's advice, and I could almost see the contented smile on Snow White's face when she received the life insurance check. I slammed on the brakes, both "foot" and "hand" and tried to "lay the bike down." Momentum carried me over the handlebars and smashed me into the trunk of the stopped vehicle. The driver unconcernedly pulled away, leaving me lying there, dazed, bloody and shaking, partly from shock, partly rage. A large, enclosed amphitheater redolent with Zyklon B is too good for the massive number of moronic drivers who take their lives (and yours) in their hands on the highways and byways of Los Angeles.

The police came and questioned me and a few bystanders, but no one had noted the license plate number of the car, and that was that. I put my shattered goggles in my pocket, thanked God I had worn my helmet and shakily approached my downed cycle again. Miraculously, it had suffered little damage. The police suggested I see a doctor immediately to be sure there were no internal injuries or broken bones. I told them I would, and then, like the damn fool I am, I got back on the bike. I have rarely, if ever, wanted more to do anything like I wanted *not* to ride the motorcycle again that afternoon, but I knew if I let even one day go by without getting back on it, I would probably never ride one again.

I found a phone and called the theater manager, who managed to find my wife. She began cursing me for being late, but lapsed into proper solicitousness when I told her about the accident. I explained I was going to call our doctor and have him look me over. She said she would leave immediately and meet me at Mount Sinai Hospital, where he was in residence that day.

I headed for the hospital at a snail's pace, giving the cars in front of me plenty of leeway. I was badly frightened, and I could not control the shaking I was experiencing. Now, as I approached Mount Sinai, my right elbow began to hurt.

By the time I had parked the cycle and walked into the building, it was excruciatingly painful. The doctor greeted me, X-rayed the arm in question and came up with a hair-line fracture of the radius.

New Year's Eve was spent in bed, gill full of codeine to alleviate the pain. On January 2, I tried to play the piano. It was pure agony. The slightest pressure on the fingers of my right hand was unbearable. I went to see a bone specialist, who began treatment by aspirating my arm—i.e., inserting a hypodermic syringe directly into the elbow and removing blood to relieve pressure on the fracture. When Goodson and Todman finally produce the inevitable quiz show, "What's Your Injury," and the panel is asked to name the ten best examples of exquisite pain, elbow-aspirating will have to rank high on the list.

Judy's choice of songs for the last show we had done should have told me of her broken romance with Glenn Ford. She had sung "Better Luck Next Time," "Almost Like Being in Love" and "This Can't Be Love." She had rarely dipped so deeply into the romantic-torch bag before. Now, as I went back to work, not having spoken to her since our last phone conversation, I wondered about her frame of mind. It did not take long to find out.

"She's not coming in," said Colleran to the assembled staff.

"Not today, you mean," said Frank Peppiatt.

"Not this week at all," was the startling reply. "Not until orchestra rehearsal Thursday night."

"What," asked John Aylesworth, with a nonbelieving laugh, "are we supposed to do about material and songs for our Lady of the Angels?"

"We go out there," replied Colleran. "Out to her house."

He cleared his throat nervously and looked down at his desk. "Matter of fact, er—that's pretty much going to be the pattern from now on, fellows. She, uh—she doesn't want to come in early in the week anymore."

"So the mountains go to Mohammed," said Gary.

"Again," I amended.

Dean Whitmore, who had replaced Bill Hobin as director, said, "There's certainly going to be a lot of wasted time and motion going to and coming from her house."

Colleran said, helplessly, "I know and I'm sorry, but that's the way it has to be. Maybe she'll change her mind in a week or so and start coming to the studio, but——"

"What time are we expected out there?" I asked.

"Around two, right after lunch."

From that day forward, a pattern was established that was unbroken until the show terminated. On Mondays, we would arrive at the Garland residence in the early afternoon. We would be treated to hors d'oeuvres, drinks and two hours or so of jokes, gossip and idle conversation. There would be impatient looks at watches by every member of the staff and blithe disregard of their impatience by Judy. We would never get around to discussing the show until late afternoon, and since she liked eating dinner late, more often than not, the meeting would not break up until eight thirty or nine at night. Already strained relationships between husbands and wives connected with the show were put to an even greater test, and the fact that a woman was putting so many grown men through the hoops, at her beck and call, subject to her whims, did not endear our guys to their respective ladies or further enhance the esteem in which the wives held them.

Judy could not have cared less. She was lonely and unhappy. She wanted company and had found a way to improve on the Dawn Patrol. Now, she was able to assemble not just a single aviator but a whole squadron. Soon our forays out to her house were stretched to two days a week, and to add to the madness, Gary and Colleran were being summoned as usual in the middle of the night. "Doesn't she ever sleep?" became the most common phrase heard around the office.

The eighteenth show was not much to write home about. Ken Murray's movie clips were interesting, but there was a dispiritedness about the whole event. Judy was feeling bitchy, and it showed up in the "Trunk" spot. She told a pointless little story about her Metro days; of how, one afternoon, after having worked hard on the set all day, she was ordered to appear before Louis B. Mayer, who informed her she would be picked up that evening at 8:00 P.M. and driven to Pasadena, where she would participate in the grand opening of a new supermarket. It did not matter that she had run the "I-was-exploited-at-MGM" bit into the ground within the internecine confines of our offices, but I felt it was ill-advised and otherwise foolish to expose her feelings to the viewing audience. Few people would find these facts interesting and, in any event, they would certainly have trouble relating to the intrigues of a motion-picture studio.

"I don't care whether you liked it or not," she snapped at me after the show. "I always swore I'd get even with Mayer, and, goddamit, now I am."

"Do you mean to tell me you really think you got even tonight? With a man who is dead and in his grave?"

"That's not the point," she parried pettishly. "Everybody

who knows what I went through with him will understand what I said, and why I said it."

"And that gives you satisfaction?"

"Damn right."

"OK, Sadie, it's your show. Look, I got pushed around at Metro the few years I was under contract out there. Not as badly as you, of course, but I got my lumps, all the same. I just don't know if I would waste valuable air time, to impress a tiny handful of 'in' people. You know damn well the average TV viewer won't know what you're talking about when that show airs."

"Screw 'em! I wanted to get it off my chest and tonight was as good a time as any."

As in the past, there was no point in discussing the matter further when she was in this kind of determined mood.

Johnny Bradford had come back to the show recently. He had, after all, originally been signed for the duration of the show. Judy and her agents admitted this. He and his agents insisted on every penny owed him. It was decided he would have to be paid, and since Garland was forced to dole out good money to him every week, he was required to be present during the week's operations. He was not permitted to write anything, contribute ideas or participate in creative discussions. At first, he approached this demeaning situation with an air of amused tolerance; but his pride and self-respect fought the good fight and won, and after a few weeks of imposed anonymity around the office, he threw up his hands in disgust and walked out. Garland's advisors pounced on his exit as a sign of his "unwillingness to cooperate," and, once again, his checks were halted. He instituted suit against Kingsrow Productions, and, as far as I know, he is still awaiting settlement.

On January 17, we taped the nineteenth show, which had a few good moments and one bad one. Louis Jourdan was our guest, and he charmingly performed a medley of "cartoon" songs with Judy ("Little Lulu," "Little Orphan Annie," "Someday My Prince Will Come"). Garland had kicked the show off to a bright start by repeating "San Francisco," and as the astronauts are wont to say, we were "looking good." As we came to the end of the show, however, she elected to repeat "Battle Hymn of the Republic." It was a classic case of poor judgment and bad timing. As moving and effective as had been her first performance of the song weeks ago, it now seemed calculated and overdone. The studio audience reaction to it was obligatory rather than spontaneously enthusiastic. Judy sensed this and admitted later it had been a bad move.

Then, on the next show, she was unaccountably dedicated to the idea of doing the one-woman concert she had wanted to do after the death of John Kennedy. Perhaps because a little more time had elapsed since the President's death, or perhaps because by that time he just did not give a damn, Aubrey did not oppose this concept. Judy was stringent about the material she wanted to sing. More graphic than any description could be, here is the actual rundown of show (tape) number twenty:

1. Prelude shots w/titles and billboard

2. *FIRST COMMERCIAL*

3. Overture.

4.   a. "SWING LOW, SWEET CHARIOT"
      b. "HE'S GOT THE WHOLE WORLD IN HIS HANDS"

5. *SECOND COMMERCIAL*

6. talk/Judy

7.
   a. "WHEN JOHNNY COMES MARCHING HOME"
      —Judy w/chorus, (off-camera)
   b. "LONG, LONG TRAIL A WINDING"
      —Judy and George Fields on Harmonica
   c. "KEEP THE HOME FIRES BURNING"
      —Judy and George Fields on Harmonica
   d. "GIVE MY REGARDS TO BROADWAY"
      —Judy
   e. "BOY OF MINE"
      —Judy and violin
   f. "MY BUDDY"
      —Judy w/chorus (off-camera)
   g. "OH, HOW I HATE TO GET UP IN THE MORNING"
      —Judy
   h. "OVER THERE" AND "GRAND OLD FLAG"
      —Judy

8. *THIRD COMMERCIAL*

9. talk and costume change—Judy

10. "THAT'S ENTERTAINMENT"
    —Judy

11.
    a. ½ hour closing billboard
    b. Station break
    c. ½ hour opening billboard

12. *FOURTH COMMERCIAL*

13. talk—Judy (about her children)
14.　a. "MAKE SOMEONE HAPPY"
　　　—Judy w/chorus (off-camera)
　　b. "LIZA"
　　　—Judy
　　c. "HAPPINESS IS JUST A THING CALLED
　　　JOE(Y)"
　　　—Judy
　　d. "LORNA'S SONG"
　　　—Judy w/chorus (off-camera)
15. *FIFTH COMMERCIAL*
16. "ROCK-A-BYE YOUR BABY WITH A DIXIE
　　　MELODY"
　　　—Judy
17. *SIXTH COMMERCIAL*
18. talk/ Judy
19. "WE'RE A COUPLE OF SWELLS"
　　　—Judy
20. talk/Judy
21. "AMERICA THE BEAUTIFUL"
　　　—Judy w/chorus (off-camera)
22. Credits
23. Closing billboard
24. Tag.

Not surprisingly, the show went extremely well. Garland knew every single song intimately. Indeed, many of them were standard concert pieces she had sung time and again. She was also overjoyed about the low-cost factor of this show. There were no sets, no dancers, few new musical arrangements to pay for. Consequently, she took a giant bite out of the money pie that week, and she loved the taste of it.

"That's what we should have done from the very beginning," she cried. "A concert show. Just me and the band, like I do on my one-night tours."

She turned a deaf ear to those among us who suggested she would run out of Judy Garland "evergreens" long before we ran out of shows to do. She was not interested in our collective opinion: a one-woman show, occasionally, departing from the standard format of a variety show was fresh and interesting, yet no one in the history of television had ever been presumptuous enough to foist themselves on the public week after week in such an intimate medium as television without the inclusion of guests, sets and a varied entertainment format.

Nonetheless, she was fascinated with the financial possibilities. This had been show number twenty. Six more and, in view of the low ratings, she would probably be canceled. She was interested in storing up nuts for the winter now. The below-the-line costs (technical facilities, stage crew, sets, graphic arts, etc.), were badly in arrears, owing to Garland's costly habit of keeping our audiences (and the stagehands, cameramen, technicians, et al.) waiting for hours while she made up, changed clothes, indulged in aimless chatter and generally sabotaged the schedule each Friday night. Often, we would end up taping our final sequences in the early hours of Saturday morning to less than half a house, the rest of the disgruntled, impatient spectators having long since made their escape. This overtime is known as "golden time," and it is aptly named. The costs incurred in such long hours are astronomical.

On the very next show, Colleran gave in to her demand to dominate the first half of the show in a "concert" vein.

Diahann Carroll and I were the guests and were not seen until well after the first half hour had gone by. This approach was neither fish nor fowl, as far as I could tell. It was not, in substance, a concert performance or a variety show but a mishmash of both and spectacularly ineffective. For weeks, my manager had been trying to get specific dates for my remaining guest shots. He had been put off, time and again, by Garland's agents, who, in turn, had their hands full with Judy and her increasing wrathfulness. She had, during the last few shows, progressed from guarded dislike of Gary Smith to open disdain, and she made no bones about it to anyone who would listen. Gary, who had been diligent and professional to a fault, was undeserving of her abuse, and most of us saw through her surface actions to the probable real cause. He represented a walking payroll she would like to do without. She was pushing hard for the one-woman shows, in a desperate bid to conserve cash. Gary was redundant. As a matter of fact, she was looking hard at everyone, shrewdly determining whom she could dispense with posthaste. Gary's number was merely the first on the board. It has been erroneously reported that Gary Smith was the last of the original television staff to be fired. Not so. He left the show now, after the twenty-first effort, and I remained.

On this show in question, I was prevailed upon by the writers and Colleran to perform a concert arrangement of "Blues in the Night." I had recorded it recently, and, to a man, they all felt it was my strongest performance material. The audience reaction to it, at the taping, was gratifying to say the least, and I caught sight of Frank and John, George Sunga, Bill Colleran and his wife Lee, among others, applauding and whistling like mad. Later that night, I attended a party given by the staff in honor of Gary and his imminent departure to New York and sanity. To no one's surprise, Judy was among the missing. At one point, Gary walked over to me, shook hands and congratulated me on my performance that evening.

"I told you 'Blues in the Night' would break it up."

"That you did, Gar. That you did."

He snorted and said, "Of course, you heard the great lady's reaction to it, didn't you?"

"No," I sighed, "but at this point, nothing would surprise me."

"Well, while everyone was cheering like the Rams had just won a game, she stuck her nose in the air and said your number was pretentious."

"Well, let's face it, it wasn't exactly 'Jingle Bells.'"

"Cut it out. You know and I know why she put the whammy on your spot tonight."

"You mean, my days are numbered, right?"

"On the button!"

"Well, what the hell, who cares? The show's days are numbered, and there aren't many numbers left."

"Gee," he said sadly, "when I think of what this show could have been."

"Hey, tiger, this is supposed to be a party. No post mortems, huh?"

Frank Peppiatt came over and clapped his huge arm around Gary. "Come on, buddy, let's go do some serious drinking."

Gary smiled at me and allowed himself to be herded toward the refreshments. Orval Payne tapped me on the shoulder. He had a glass in his hand, which he now raised in salute to me. "Beautiful tonight, Mel. Just great."

"Thank you, Orval."

"Too bad about Gary."

"I don't know. I think he's better off, somehow."

He gave me a knowing look. "You're next, you know."

"It figures."

He took a sip of his drink. "The bitch. No one ever really knows where they stand with her."

"How long have you been doing her hair, Orval?"

"Too long! Too damn long!"

"She certainly seems to like you."

"It varies. She changes, like the wind. One minute she loves you, the next she'll cut your balls off."

He took another drink. "Yeah, she's a real ball-breaker, that woman. She loves to see people fired. Gives her a feeling of power, you know? Take George Schlatter, for instance."

"Well, you can't blame his firing on Garland. I mean, everyone knows——"

"Crap! Everyone knows nothing! Aubrey didn't fire Schlatter. Garland fired him! I was there, with her, in the room, when she gave the orders to can him. She got CBS to take the rap, because she didn't want to be the heavy; but take my word it was all Judy's idea!"

I was stunned by this bit of news, but only momentarily. I had always known what a great actress she was. Now, all her breast-beating and tooth-gnashing over George leaving the show came back to me, and I knew suddenly that Orval was telling the truth.

Later on, I found out Judy had taken the late flight to New York that very evening, for another week-long vacation. If Television City was the Land of the Gargoyles, then

New York was Oz and Jilly's was the Home of the Wizard. And it was during that week, one night, at Jilly's, that something happened to Judy that would shortly cause her to spell finis to our association.

Chapter 9

Bill Colleran looked awful. His complexion was the color of club soda and there was about him an air of bewilderment, as if he had gotten out of bed that morning, looked in the mirror and said to himself, "What, in God's name, is happening?" Apparently the rigors of producing "The Judy Garland Show" were not even slightly relieved by the past week's vacation. He also looked embarrassed. As I sat in his office, he managed to move every item on his desk in a sort of compulsory-neatness game he was playing with himself. As he spoke, he touched on a variety of mundane subjects: the weather, the condition of his car's engine, the sniffles one of his children was experiencing—all these he gabbed about nervously as he practiced avoiding my eyes by scrutinizing the window, walls and other sundry objects in the office. Eventually, he got to it.

"We, uh—" he began, clearing his throat, "we've got a little problem."

"Oh? I say 'Oh,' because I can't think of anything wittier to say just now."

He shot a helpless look at me, then said, to his knees, "Yes, well, the fact is, Judy, uh—Judy, as you know, was in New York again last week, and, uh—one night, in Jilly's——"

"Where else?"

"—one night in Jilly's, she heard this fellow play and sing—and she liked what she heard——"

"I'll just bet she did."

"—so much so that she—she's brought this guy back to California with her——"

"Ah-hah! Something new has been added."

"Er—yes. Not just to her own personal life, but to the show. She wants us—she's *told* us to find something for him to do on the show. She says he's a great musician and composer. Maybe he could help you write special material?" His inflection ended on a high note of hopefulness.

"And what, pray tell, is the name of this young genius? I assume, of course, that he is young and pretty."

"His name's Bobby Cole. Know him?"

"I met him once." He had been playing in a small bar in New York a few years back. I had gone in with some friends for a late drink and listened to a young, dark-haired man of medium height sing all the predictable Rodgers and Hart, Jerome Kern, Harold Arlen songs that seem to be "musts" among the ranks of the piano-bar performers. He played well enough, and his singing was pleasant if not impressive. I told Colleran so. He shook his head in slight annoyance, as if he did not wish to discuss it any further; Judy imposes and we disposes.

"We have to add him to the staff and that's that."

"Uh-huh. What about billing? On the show, in the credits?"

"I'll think of something. Assistant special-material writer, something like that, OK?"

"Not on your tintype."

"What?"

"I said, no, not OK."

"Look, you don't understand——"

"I understand perfectly. I realize I haven't got a prayer as far as having anything to say about this. It's Judy's show. She has the right to hire anyone she wants. But for Christ's sake, Bill, don't look me in the eye and ask me if it's OK. You knew the answer to that all along."

He nodded his head, rubbing his eyes with his hand. "Sure I knew, but what can I do about it? Judy has a *thing* for this guy, all of a sudden. And Mel, I have to be fair with you, she's also suddenly got a—*thing* about you. What happened on the last show? Did you and she have words or something?"

I smiled. "No, we didn't, but I've been expecting something like this to happen."

"Really? Why?"

"Let's just say the writing's been on the wall for over a month now. It's really very simple to figure out. Supply and demand."

Colleran had no idea of what I was talking about, and frankly, I was only one step ahead of him. I was punchy with fatigue, having battled with Snow White continually for the past four days, during which time our marriage had fallen to the very bottom of the ladder, bumping its chin against every single rung on the way down. Now, like a couple of battered boxers, we were sitting warily in our respective corners, deciding whether it was worth it to come out for another, final round or simply to call it a draw. In my condition that morning, I was not in the mood to be understanding about Judy's latest find. Colleran got up and paced.

"This is the trickiest situation I've ever been up against," he confided. "Just before you walked in here, I was on the long-distance phone with Bobby Cole's wife. Are you ready for this? She called to tell me she's pregnant and that this is the first time she and Bobby have ever had trouble. I had to sit here and listen to that poor girl cry her heart out to me."

"What did you say to her?"

"What could I say? She kept pleading with me to send him home. How do you send a grown man home to his wife if he wants to be somewhere else?"

"I don't know, Mr. Anthony, I just don't know."

"Please, Mel," he appealed to me once again. "Find something for this guy to do, will you?"

"Bill," I asked, not wanting to answer him directly just yet, "we only have a few shows to go. Now I have a contract for two more guest shots, and so far, my manager has not been able to pin them down. I want to know, here and now, where I stand as far as those shots are concerned."

He shrugged. "You know Judy. When she decides to——"

"You mean, *if* she decides, don't you?"

"All right, if she decides to honor the commitment, you'll do the two guest shots."

"Otherwise?"

"Otherwise, I guess you'll just have to sue her or something."

I got up. "Right. You're a very nice guy, Bill, and I realize you have very little control over what's going on at this point, so I'm not going to be rude or discourteous to you. Since we're nearly at the end of this little charade we've all been playing, it makes very little difference to me who Judy wants to play house with, even if it means employing him on the show; but I have survived three separate regimes, and I've managed to avoid being degraded by her. I'm sure that for financial reasons alone, she would like me to quit, because she hasn't got a hope in hell of firing me, and she knows it. Now at this moment, I want to quit so bad I can taste it. But she's going to have to do it the hard way and find some way to can me, 'cause that's the only way I'm going."

Colleran started to speak, thought better of it and kept silent.

"Now, Bill, one more thing. As of now, I am going to do what I was originally hired to do; write music and lyrics. I will be in my office at all times, available when I'm needed."

"You mean, you're not going to work on the stage with Judy anymore?"

"I wasn't hired to in the first place. I did it as a favor and she knows it. Now that she's gotten around to pressure plays with me, I'm fresh out of favors. Hey! How about Bobby Cole taking over that job? Now that would make sense."

"I don't know," he said, perturbed. "I don't know how Judy's going to take this."

"Frankly, Scarlett, I don't give a damn. And if that isn't an exit line, I never heard one."

I left Bill sitting there and went into my office.

Subconsciously, I had known it would come to this. Perhaps it was just as well. My marriage was in its death throes. My position on the show had been tenuous for some time now. Judy's acerbic critique of my last appearance on the show was proof enough for me that the spearmint had lost its flavor. I was suddenly impatient wtih her chameleonlike nature. Aw, what the hell, Melvin, I thought. Give up the ghost. Pack your electric pencil sharpener and stalk off into the night. On the other hand, I argued with myself, we're talking about relinquishing a lot of money. You haven't a thing lined up in the way of other guest shots or nightclub engagements. Are you going to surrender all that dough to The Legend, not to mention the television exposure you would be giving up via the pair of guest shots she owes you? If you stick around, it's going to be a contest of wills, you know that. Are you up to it? Is it worth it? And what of young Master Cole?

My thoughts turned to him for a moment. All right, be fair, Tormé. Can you really blame him? Look at the whole picture realistically:

Night after night, he sits at a piano in a side-street bistro, banging his head against the solid wall of noise that is characteristic of every boite of that ilk—playing good songs for deaf people, tuned-out Johns on the make for the girl on the next stool, high-priced hustlers looking to score big with some aging, out-of-town Lothario who thinks because he is *here,* actually *here* at Jilly's where the stars hang out, he is automatically "in," "hip," "with it."

And then there are those nights when Frank Sinatra, The Pope himself, graces Jilly's with his presence, surrounded by his phalanx of cronies, groovy-looking chicks sticking to him like brambles; and in the corner of the room, trying to make himself heard over the din and seen through the smoke is Bobby Cole, craning his neck occasionally for a look at Frank and wishing to God it was he at the long table, adored, admired, respected, affluent, desirable.

And so one night, Judy Garland, another show-biz heavy-weight, flounces in, and for a change he *is* the object of rapt attention, at least where Judy is concerned. When he finishes singing, he is invited to her table and treated with respect and affection. Then, amazingly, she is asking him to come with her to California, to work on her television show. (It is like a bad movie. Things like this just don't happen in real life—didn't he just see this plot on "The Late Late Show"—Alice Faye and John Payne, wasn't it?) But no, this is for real! Judy loves his work and is offering him a job. Suddenly the hundreds of nights of inhaling other people's cigarette smoke, of being ingratiating to drunken broads who eye him invitingly, their breasts popping from low-cut dresses, preposterous little lipstick-smeared grins on their faces, all this is wiped away, and ahead lies Hollywood, Playground of the Stars, fabled land of plenty, and he is being asked to go and go first-cabin.

Only the crassest of moralists could blame Bobby Cole for taking advantage of this once-in-a-lifetime opportunity. Everyone, including myself, was taking for granted the fact that he was Judy's new amour. There was no proof as yet that such was the case. Perhaps it was purely business. Perhaps Judy was on a star-making kick. Perhaps after all she honestly fell down over his performance one night at Jilly's, and . . .

It ought to be interesting from here on in, I speculated. I'm going to stick around and see what happens. As it turned out, that wasn't for very long.

Peppiatt and Aylesworth took me to lunch and tried to prognosticate.

"Maybe it won't be so bad, working with this Bobby Cole guy," said John. "Why not give it a try?"

"I've been all through that, John. It's not just Bobby Cole. It's—everything. We've only got a few more to do, and——"

"That's exactly the point. There are only a couple of shows left, and——"

"—why not hang in there," interrupted Frank, "and finish them, all of us, together?"

"Hey, you guys, I can't tell you how much I appreciate your concern. And your friendship——"

"Hell, Number One, what would action in the North Atlantic be without you?"

"—but I'm kind of fed up. With everything."

"What's happening on the home front?"

"John, there just isn't any home front at this point. Everything's hitting the fan at once."

"I'm sorry to hear that."

Frank said, "Anything we can do?"

"Well, if you know any secret formulas for saving a dead marriage or convincing Garland I'm irreplaceable——"

"What are you going to do now? I mean right now?"

"Well, I'm going to finish this excellent lunch you just bought me, and then I'm going up to my office and wait to see what happens."

"She's not going to sit still for you not working down on the stage with her, you know that."

"Maybe. Maybe not. But take my word, I've waved my arms around on that stage for the last time."

Frank squinted at me. "You really want out, don't you?"

"I think what I want is pretty irrelevant, don't you? Judy is looking to save money now. I represent a healthy chunk of dough she could pocket from now until the show goes off the air. Do you realize how much money has been wasted on overtime, discarded arrangements, hell, whole segments we've tossed out, sets and all? I wouldn't be surprised if every single show went over the $140,000 mark. Way over. God, what a waste! Now all of a sudden Judy realizes the end is in sight, and she's got to recoup, anyway she can. It's simple arithmetic. I'm just not going to lift one finger to help her pick my pocket."

"But isn't refusing to direct her on stage the kiss of death for you?" asked John.

"Not really. She knows and I know that that little service was not part of our deal. She hasn't got a leg to stand on in that department."

"OK," warned Frank, "but she'll find a way."

"Oh, I have no doubt of that, Captain. I'm fascinated to see just how she manages it."

When I returned to my office, I called Colleran.

"Hi, Bill," I said brightly. "Just wanted you to know I'm back from lunch and ready to write anything Judy might need for the show."

"Oh. Uh—gee, Mel, I don't know just what she has in mind this week."

"No problem, Bill," I answered, and then, more pointedly, said, "I just wanted you to know where I am. I'm in my office, manuscript pen poised and ready. And Bill?"

"Yes?"

"I'm not leaving until you call and dismiss me for the day. Matter of fact, that's going to be my routine every day from now on, so I'll be checking into the office daily at around ten in the morning and going to lunch around noontime, and after that, I'll be here all day until I'm either needed or dismissed. OK?"

He expelled his breath. "OK, Mel," he answered softly. I felt sorry for him.

"Hey, Bill?"

"Yes?"

"We'll both survive this."

"Want to bet?" He hung up.

Later that afternoon, Judy sent word she wanted to see me. I went down to the trailer. She wasted no time on amenities.

"Jack Jones is on the show again this week, as you know."

"Yes. There, but for the Grace of God——"

"What?"

"Nothing, nothing."

She eyed me imperiously. "I haven't the time or the patience for funny *shticks* today. I want you to put together a medley of songs that Jeanette MacDonald and Nelson Eddy sang in their movies. For Jack and me."

"All right."

She smiled coldly. "It will be a nice contrast to his solo spot. I understand he's picked a couple of fine tunes to do, like that little jazz waltz he just recorded. What's it called?"

"You mean 'Wives and Lovers'?"

"That's it. Nobody sings jazz like him. Nobody."

I smiled back at her. "Your memory's failing, Sadie. We've played this game before."

"I haven't forgotten. And the rules haven't changed since then, either. Don't forget it."

I was all out of biting badinage. "Fine. You've made your point. Anything else?"

"No, that's all."

I opened the door of the trailer and started to walk away. Behind me, Judy's voice called out. "Just a minute. There is one more thing."

I stopped in my tracks, turned slowly and went back inside. Whether she had done this purposely or not, the "game" was telling on my nerves, not to mention my temper.

"What is this crap I've been hearing about you not wanting to work on the stage with me anymore?"

"I never said I didn't want to. I merely said I wouldn't."

"You realize," she said, looking victorious, "that's a breach of your contract."

"Uh-uh. No way. Read it yourself. I was hired as a writer, not a vocal conductor."

"But you've been conducting me on stage for months. You set a precedent. That's as good as having it in writing that you're supposed to function in that capacity."

"My, aren't we well-informed and spewing legal jargon all over the place."

"Never mind that," she snapped. "I want your keester on that stage."

"You'll have to ask me nicely. No, wait a minute, never mind, I didn't mean that. I'm not going to work on the stage with you anymore, and that's final."

"Fine," she smirked, "you know what that means."

"No, I want you to say it."

"All right. You're fired."

I laughed. "If you're waiting for me to say, 'You can't fire me; I quit,' you can relax. I'm not going to say it, and I'm not going to quit, and incidentally, I don't think I have given you any legal grounds to fire me, in spite of what your attorneys may have told you."

"Get out of here, you son-of-a-bitch!"

"With pleasure. I'll be upstairs, working on the medley. Any little thing I can do for you———"

"Up yours."

I left then, hating myself all the way up to my office. I had allowed myself to get snotty. That was not only stupid; it was fruitless with Judy. She had obviously been drinking and had primed herself for our confrontation. Perhaps she had hoped I would quit in anger or disgust, thereby saving her unnecessary tribulation, not to mention a tidy sum of money. The fact that I was prepared to be obstinate about giving up many thousands of dollars hit her where she was now living: right in the bank balance. It was one more frustrating thing that had not gone right for her.

I called my manager. "Joe," I said, "Judy just tried to fire me, but I refused to go. I'm still here, in the office."

I filled him in on the details.

"Melvin," he said, in his curiously gruff-yet-gentle croaking bass, "you did the correct thing. If they want you, they know where to find you, right? You've offered to write anything they need, and that's all they can ask of you. As far as working on the stage is concerned, you don't have to. That's not what they're paying you for. What they're paying you for is the writing of special material and," he added bitterly, "two more guest shots, which they are obviously not going to schedule, in spite of your contract."

I was tired. A sudden headache now pounded behind my eyeballs. "I don't know, Joe. Is it worth it? Judy wants to get rid of me, and frankly, I want out just as badly."

"You want to give up all that money? Didn't you tell me you and your wife are up for grabs?"

"Yeah, we've just about had it."

"Well, babe, you're going to need that dough. All of it. At this moment 'The Judy Garland Show' is your main source of income. I'm working on some dates out of town for you, but for the next month or so, I want you to stay put there at CBS."

"Well, I don't know——"

"Do this my way, Melvin. Believe me, you won't be sorry."

I hung up and looked at the four walls. It was late in the afternoon. The February sun was dying, and the office seemed cheerless and cold. I turned the heat up, went to the piano and put together a batch of Eddy-MacDonald songs. When I had finished the work and had made a lead sheet in the proper keys for Jack and Judy, I informed Colleran of its completion, and he had it picked up.

Then I just sat there and waited.

And waited.

I looked around to find myself sitting in the dark. My watch said eight o'clock. I had not heard from Colleran and could only guess that either everybody had gone home or they were still down in the rehearsal hall. I dialed the number. No answer. I called Colleran's office, the writers' department, Stage 43. A guard answered and said the stage was empty. I was suddenly overcome with depression. I did not want to go home and face another evening of wrangling with my wife. The day's events were still unresolved, and I felt like the forgotten man. I thought of going over to the City Slicker. Maybe John and Frank would be there and . . .

Instead, I drove to a drive-in theater, had a hamburger and slept through a pair of lousy horror movies. When I got home, the house was silent. Tracy was asleep in his bedroom, and when I tried the door to mine, it was locked. I was relieved. I tiptoed to the guest room, and, after a maddening few hours of going over everything that had occurred during the day, I drifted into a troubled sleep and dreamed a grotesque nightmare in which both Judy and my wife were trying to run me down in the street with their respective cars.

Colleran looked wiped out when I saw him the next morning. He had been on Dawn Patrol duty the previous night, and Judy had been unusually stormy. A good portion of her ire was directed at me, said Colleran, and he had been unable to calm her down or cope with her violent outbursts. I did not ask if Bobby Cole had been on hand. If he had, and Colleran wanted me to know, he would have ventured the information.

"Jesus," exclaimed Colleran. "She was in one hell of a state. What did you say to her yesterday?"

"I merely told her what I told you, Bill. I'm through working down on the stage, in front of the audience. You know why. For that matter, everyone around here knows why. Even Judy. Let's face it, she's looking for a good reason to fire me. If I had agreed to continue the vocal conducting, she would have found another way to go."

"She tells me she did fire you. Yesterday afternoon, in the trailer. But you refused to leave."

"That's right."

He threw his hands up in the air. "God, I don't know what to tell you. She's—she's very down on you. Very down."

"Funny how quickly that happened, isn't it? One moment we were getting along like bandits and the next, or to be precise, within one week's time, I'm suddenly the heavy. Marvelous!"

"Well, you know Judy——"

"No, I don't. I don't believe anyone knows her. She doesn't even know herself. Would you believe me if I told you something surprising?"

"Nothing could surprise me these days."

"I'm not angry with the lady. For a few minutes yesterday, I nearly lost my temper with her, but in the cold light of today, the whole situation seems terribly sad. I've seen Judy behave erratically, but it's obvious she's a lot more disturbed than any of us ever realized. Now, you couple that troubled nature with brilliant talent, a great sense of humor and occasional glimmers of humanity, and you got the damnedest tiger-by-the-tail in the history of women."

He looked me in the eye. "Well, where do we go from here?"

"I don't know about you, Kingfish, but I'm going back into my office. I've played this record before, but lest you forget: I will be available to write anything that is required of me, at any time. I want to also remind you it's getting very late in the day for my guest shots."

He grunted, "Forget about them, Mel. She's not going to give them to you."

"I know. I just wanted to hear somebody say it out loud. She's going to have to pay me for them, you know, whether or not I do them."

Colleran could only shrug. I got a funny thought just then. I wondered, statistically, how many times members of the Garland crew had shrugged, grunted, grimaced, sputtered, stuttered, fumed, gasped and otherwise looked helpless since we had begun the show, twenty thousand light-years ago, last June.

The rest of the week staggered on, slowly unwinding like

a slithering python. The medley I had written was only partially used, having been "rewritten" by—someone. I laughed when I heard that phrase, "rewritten." "Beautiful!" I said to Frank and John. "How the hell do you 'rewrite' Romberg, Friml and Victor Herbert?"

Thursday night, I was summoned to band call. Very little of what I had put together was being used, but since some of my handiwork was retained, I felt Garland was well within her rights to call on me. The show was to be a modified concert again, with Judy dominating most of the hour. Jack Jones and a Ken Murray film segment were spotted just prior to the "Trunk" spot. When Jack and Judy sang the MacDonald-Eddy duet, I scarcely recognized it, and when she faltered over a certain passage, she motioned for me to come into the bandroom.

"What the hell is this *thing* I'm singing here?" she asked, pointing to the music in her hand.

"I really couldn't say, Judy," I answered quietly, determined to keep calm no matter what.

"What do you mean, you don't know? You arranged it, didn't you?"

"Not all of it."

"But you *did* write most of it."

"No, just a small part of what's on that sheet."

"Well, then who——"

"I don't know." She knew damn well "who."

"Correct me if I'm wrong; wasn't it your job to put this medley together? Didn't I tell you to?"

"You certainly did."

"Then why is it all different from the way I saw it last Tuesday? What happened?"

"Mice?" I ventured.

"Don't be a smart ass, Tormé."

"I can't vouch for the 'smart' part."

She slapped the sheet of music with her hand. "Well, what am I supposed to do about this? It's rotten."

"Gee, I'd sure like to help, Judy. Any suggestions?"

"Yes, I have one, but you wouldn't take it."

I turned to Colleran. "I'm going up to my office. If I don't hear from you by ten o'clock, I'm going home." Without another word, I left the bandroom and headed upstairs, determined to end this nonsense once and for all. Pride is a stern jailer sometimes. No matter how hard you try to fight it, if you are stuck with it and its bunkmate, self-respect, it will always come back to kick you in the teeth and have the final upper hand. Judy had played the verbal-emasculation game well tonight, demeaning me in front of the musicians, every single one of whom I knew, most of whom respected me as a singer, musician and arranger; they had, in fact, almost to a man, worked on many of my recording dates. Now, finally, I was resolute, lost revenue or no lost revenue.

Automatically, I began to clean out my desk. As surely as I was standing in an office at CBS Television City, I knew the phone would ring any moment. The third floor was deserted, silent. Even so, the jangling of the telephone on my desk did not startle me. I picked it up.

"Mel? Bill."

"Yeah, Bill, I know."

"Judy—Judy wants you out of that office—uh—out of the building, as a matter of fact."

Here it was. Oddly enough, while I had been expecting this, I found it hard to swallow. I had never been fired, dismissed or rejected professionally before. Perhaps it's good for the soul, this new experience, I thought. Perhaps, like a novitiate, I had become too self-loving, too prideful, and God or fate or Mother Superior Garland was giving me a taste of the cat on my back. Tempted as I was to wear a hairshirt at that moment, common sense prevailed. This was simply the natural order of things, and to take it personally would have been foolish.

"Okay, Bill. No sweat. I'll be out of here in fifteen minutes."

"Mel, I'm sorry."

"Forget it. The mills of the Gods, you know?"

"If you mean what I think you mean, I wish you the best of luck."

I gathered up my junk and made my way down the empty corridor to the elevator. It was just after nine when I emerged into the cold, fresh air. I felt light-headed, realized I had not eaten for hours and stopped in at Canter's delicatessen on Fairfax for a sandwich and a think. Reaction was setting in. It was over and done with. Straight ahead now. At that moment I wanted to talk to someone. But to whom? Should I go home? Negative. There was no home, just a house with furniture and paintings and assorted gimcracks and a marriage that had slipped its moorings and was listing heavily, all but sunk, and a little boy I loved but had neglected for months in favor of work and my futile attempts to solidify the situation between his mother and myself. Should I bare my soul to Joe Shribman? Time enough tomorrow, when we would jointly decide what action to take re the money owed me by Kingsrow Productions. And now as I sat alone in the large, brightly lighted restaurant, watching the comings and goings of the patrons—*alte bubbies* noshing away at cream cheese and lox on bagels or onion rolls; teen-agers laughing loudly in a booth, tapping their feet and drumming on the table to some unheard tune they secretly shared; six ladies at the next table, scanning the menus, talking weight-watcher talk and reliving the evening's card game; a rabbi in his orthodox working clothes, complete with *payes,* long beard and traditional hat, incongruously leering over the bakery counter at a bin of elaborate danish, inviting his lady companion to choose what she fancied; several complete families, all generations represented from gnarled old grandpas and grandmas to the middle-aged sons and daughters-in-law (or vice versa) to the young elementary-school children, rosy-cheeked from the night air and insatiable in their appetites to the new-born babes and toddlers, goggle-eyed in their strollers, mesmerized by the gabble and the laughter and the lights and the clanking and clinking of glasses, knives, forks, spoons, dishes—as I watched, I suddenly realized I couldn't think of a single person I wanted to speak to, confide in, seek solace from, use as a sounding board. And like that old device you have seen so many times in films where the protagonist is suddenly lost in thought in the middle of a crowd and his reverie magically obliterates all the noise, all the sound around him, I found myself in a cocoon of self-imposed silence, the hubbub of the restaurant blocked out, and I felt like an antecedent of Buck Rogers, in a state of suspended animation.

In slow motion, I paid my bill, oozed out the door like a wisp of ectoplasm and started driving. I wound up at the beach. I got out of the car, made my way out to the sand and sat down, looking roughly toward Hawaii. I suppose, subconsciously, I felt I appeared a tragic figure, staring out over the timeless sea. No doubt a strange girl, herself alone and misunderstood and unhappy, would walk by, barefoot and beautiful. She would stop, look back at me, her long golden hair blowing in the wind, and suddenly we would be huddled together, co-conspirators against loneliness, trading confidences, exploring each other's eyes; and incredibly she would be that girl I had always looked for and dreamed about, the perfect girl, wise, not clever, lovely as opposed to exotically beautiful, wonderfully desirable, not calculatingly sexy.

The ocean air was chilly and the wind cut through my bones. You *have* seen too many movies, Melvin. There is no girl, no romance, no solution here. Just an empty, cold beach, a knife-edged gale and your unromantic runny nose. I got back into the car, called home and informed Snow White I was checking into a motel, which was fine with her.

I met Shribman in my lawyer's office bright and early the next day. I presented the facts as simply and accurately as possible. The first thing to be done was to lock up the money owed me. My attorney got a court injunction issued, which ordered CBS to place the complete amount of salary owed me for writing and performing into a kind of escrow. I could not touch it, but neither could Garland or her associates. Eventually we would go to court and arbitrate, and, my lawyer felt sure, I would receive most or all of what was coming in the way of payment.

Later I had coffee with Joe and told him I wanted to go to work out of town immediately.

"I don't think that's a good idea, Mel. In actuality, our position is this; Judy illegally broke a contract with you. You are still here in town, ready to work if she calls you, until the last show is done. If you're out of town and her agents hear about it and get the bright idea to call you in to work, because they know you're not available, that could be a breach of contract on your part. No, you gotta stick around, at least until the twenty-sixth show is finished."

I was miserable. "What am I supposed to do with myself?"

"Why not use this time to do some writing? Songwriting, I mean."

"Frankly, Joe, I just don't feel like it. Now that I haven't got an office, the only piano available to me is at home, and, at this point, the less time I spend there, the better for all concerned."

"Well, tiger, I don't know what to tell you, but I guarantee you, if you leave town now, you can kiss all that money good-by."

So I stayed.

On Saturday morning the phone rang. I picked it up and was taken totally unawares by the sound of Judy's voice, exasperation bordering each measured word.

"We taped a show last night, or didn't you know that?"

"Of course I knew it."

"Well, where the hell were you? You weren't there when I needed you."

"Oh? You needed me?"

"You're supposed to be the musical supervisor of this show, aren't you?"

"Yes I am. Or was, until Thursday night when you issued your eviction notice."

"*Who* issued *what* eviction notice?"

"Cut it out, Judy. I am tired of the game."

"Come on, don't avoid the subject. What's with this 'eviction notice' bit?"

"All right. You've just got to have it spelled out, haven't you? I don't know whether you're recording this on tape for posterity's sake, but since you need to have me say it, I'm happy to oblige. Thursday evening after you neatly castrated me in front of several dozen people, I went back to my office, received a call from Colleran, who told me, as per your instructions, to get out of the building. Now correct me if I'm wrong."

As deftly as Elroy Hirsch, she swivel-hipped her way around that one.

"All I know is, you weren't there when I needed you, and I can't pay people who won't do their work."

"Hey, lady, are you deaf? I asked you a question. Did you or did you not order Colleran to tell me to get out?"

Doggedly, as if by rote, she repeated the same broken-record line: "All I know is, you weren't there when I needed you, and I cannot pay people who won't do their work. So you're fired."

"Good Christ. Aren't you getting tired of firing me? That's the third time in ten days."

"Yeah," she replied laconically. "Third time's the charm. Maybe it'll stick this time." She hung up without another word.

I lived at home for the next few weeks, and by unspoken agreement, my wife and I avoided each other as much as possible. It was a strain on both of us and a disturbing puzzle to Tracy, who could not understand why his mother and father did not speak to each other anymore.

If I had ever doubted the friendships I had entered into during the past eight and one-half months, those doubts were quickly dispelled. "Out of sight, out of mind" was not being practiced by Frank and John, or George Sunga, who had remained constant throughout the whole of our relationship. Their thoughtful and cheering phone calls kept me abreast of what was happening on "The Judy Garland

Show." Tape number twenty-three, predictably, was a total concert presentation, once again devoid of sets, guests, dancers, singers or a plethora of expensive new orchestrations. The audience had been kept waiting an inordinate amount of time, even for the Garland show. Bill Colleran was talking to himself. Everyone was walking on eggs, and the new game being played around the old stamping grounds was "Avoid meetings with Garland whenever possible."

Show 24. Another concert. Vic Damone assists, but once again, no production values to speak of, no cast in evidence.

Number 25. A concert show, naturally. Bobby Cole is the guest. (He is billed as "Robert" Cole.) He sings with and plays piano for Judy. I am told he does a nice job of it and that he has deported himself with dignity and tact in the delicate situation in which he finds himself.

On March 13, 1964, the twenty-sixth and final Judy Garland show was taped. This was a total concert program, with no guests whatsoever. I was curious and interested to learn how it had gone.

Luckily, rather detailed notes were made of that last night's taping, and I was given the opportunity to examine them thoroughly. From all I was able to glean from them, I have put together a reasonably accurate picture of the final Judy Garland show.

The taping took place on Friday, March 13, 1964. Everything started rather smoothly at 11:00 A.M. The technical crew went through their paces, and Judy was represented by proxy (the usual "sing-in" girl). Consequently, by 6:00 P.M. all was in readiness for the only pretaped number on the show, "Where Is the Clown?" The audience was waiting in the hallway and on the outside ramp. At exactly six-thirty, they were ushered in. Most of them were recognized as regulars; and they exuded a general air of melancholy, since most of them realized this was the end of the road not only for the show but possibly for Judy's television career.

They sat patiently for forty-five minutes, speculating on what she would sing and say on this last evening. Then, at seven-fifteen, a harried Bill Colleran made his uncertain way onto the stage and, with obvious embarrassment, announced, "Miss Garland does not want anyone in the audience during the taping of "Where Is the Clown?" There was a minimum amount of groaning from the audience. They were, after all, regulars, and they were used to "delays and surprises." Many got up and left, while others were ushered into another studio to watch a taping of a game show, "Stump the Stars."

At approximately eight-fifteen, Judy arrived on stage in costume and makeup. She was extremely nervous and irritable. It was no secret she had dreaded doing this last show. ("It figures. She knows after tonight there's no more trailer, no more yellow-brick road, no more TV show.") In twenty-five minutes, the number was camera-blocked, and at eight-forty, it was decided to rehearse it once more "on tape." The cameras rolled, but it was a waste of time, Judy simply had not rehearsed the song adequately. It was suggested that a little additional staging might cover up some of the defects.

At nine twenty-five, the first "official" take was attempted. It was no good. The cameras rolled immediately, and by nine thirty-eight, the second take was completed. This one was somewhat better, but the last eight bars were unusable. Again, the cameras rolled, and a "pickup" of the defective eight bars was accomplished.

The start of the regular concert was to have begun at nine-thirty. It was now ten-thirty. Colleran decided to bring

the audience back in while Judy was still in her clown outfit. Since "Where Is the Clown?" would serve as the closing
number of the show, Garland could make her final speech
(still in clown makeup and wardrobe) and the closing
credits could also be shot. This was done by eleven twenty,
at which time the audience was asked to take a break while
Judy repaired to her trailer for a costume change.

Nearly one hour later, a restive audience was invited
back into the studio, but since Judy was not ready to begin
the concert, time was killed by running a video-tape play-
back of the Bobby Cole spot from show twenty-five, Liza
Minelli singing, "You Are for Loving," from show number
three, aeons ago, and the clown number they had just seen
Judy perform.

Garland was up-tight. A blind man could see she had
been drinking, that she was indescribably unhappy, that she
would have given her soul to be somewhere, anywhere except on Stage 43 that night. She called Bill Colleran into the
trailer and issued a pronouncement. Bill listened, sighed and
went to bring the word to the weary regulars. "Ladies and
gentlemen, due to—er—technical and union problems, we
will not be able to continue the show."

Now the groans were louder and sharper. The spectators
rose slowly and shuffled out, disgruntlement plainly written
on their faces. Colleran then announced to one and all that
the show was in a state of flux, and that, shortly, he would
return to the stage to let everyone know what would happen
next.

A truck from Matteo's arrived at 12:30 A.M. and began
setting up tables and food on an adjoining stage—Stage 33
—an "end of series" party having been ordered by Judy.
Since the mood was anything but festive and the remainder

of the night uncertain at best, it was deemed advisable at this juncture to feed the stagehands, technicians, orchestra members and others connected with the show. Judy remained tightly shut up in her trailer, incommunicado for the moment.

Colleran knocked on her door, and after a few seconds of silence decided she was either ignoring the knock, sleeping or had gone home. He was about to turn away when she acknowledged his presence and asked him to come in. Whatever transpired then is known only to Colleran, but somehow he persuaded her to continue.

At 2:14 A.M., Judy appeared on stage to begin the show from the top. She stopped in her tracks when she saw there were still a number of people occupying seats in the audience section and was about to storm off the stage when Colleran advised her that the fifty-odd souls in attendance were hardcore fans who had seen every single show in the series and had pleaded for the privilege of remaining just in case Judy decided to continue. He then suggested to Garland that it would be detrimental to her image and, perhaps, future career to banish such loyal followers from the court. For once, Garland listened and agreed, and this faithful, hardy band of loyalists was allowed to stay.

The concert proceeded. There were repeated delays, retakes, stops and goes, and what finally emerged at 5:54 A.M. was a mélange of bits and pieces, some usable but much of it worthless. Judy abruptly left the stage, as Colleran, looking like a finalist in a marathon dance contest, proclaimed hoarsely that she was unable to continue. Even if everything had gone perfectly, the show still would have been five minutes short.

(In the final analysis, the twenty-sixth show was made up

of material Judy had performed previously, and though some of what she sang on the evening of the last taping was used, the complete closing segment of the show—over twenty minutes' worth—was lifted right out of show number twenty-two. "Where Is the Clown?" was deleted and never shown.)

Judy's farewell speech, just prior to the closing song spot on this final program, is interesting, to say the least. Here it is, verbatim:

CLOSING TALK   *CLOSING TALK*

MUSIC: *"BORN IN A TRUNK"*

(PUSH IN ON JUDY)

JUDY

I WOULD LIKE TO TAKE A MOMENT IF
I MAY TO MENTION THAT THIS IS MY
LAST TELEVISION SHOW . . . MY LAST
SHOW OF THIS SERIES. SOME OF YOU
MAY KNOW THAT. I WILL BE DOING
CONCERTS, HOWEVER, IN THE ORIENT
AND, OF COURSE, HERE AT HOME
IF YOU WOULD LIKE.
I LOVE DOING CONCERTS MORE THAN
ANYTHING ELSE. I SUPPOSE IT'S
NOT ONLY THE ACTUAL CONTACT WITH
A GREAT MANY PEOPLE THAT MAKES
IT SO ENJOYABLE . . . BUT ALSO THAT
THE WORKING PREMISE IS A LITTLE
DIFFERENT. BY THAT, I MEAN YOU
RELY UPON YOUR INSTINCTS AND
EXPERIENCES AND AT THE RISK OF
SOUNDING OUTRAGEOUSLY IMMODEST,
IT SEEMS TO HAVE WORKED RATHER

WELL IN THE PAST AND I'M GLAD.
SO I WANT TO THANK YOU WONDERFUL
PEOPLE HERE TONIGHT FOR YOUR
SUPPORT AND THANK YOU FOR ALLOWING
ME TO LITERALLY INVADE YOUR HOMES
EVERY WEEK. I HOPE YOU FEEL IT
WAS WORTH IT. I DO.
GOODBYE FOR A WHILE.

(Over on the Paramount lot, Ben Cartwright, Hoss and Little Joe went through their daily paces, routing rustlers, punching cattle, solving the problems of the Old West, the same old routine. If they missed reading the "trades" at lunch that day, they were probably unaware of the passing of "The Judy Garland Show.")

In a widely quoted letter from James Aubrey to Judy, she was informed of the cancelation of her show. It has been reported that Aubrey also wrote, somewhat platitudinously, "The tube will not shine as brightly with you off the air. No one has ever fulfilled a commitment with more dedication or more integrity."

Since Judy's vitriolic comments about Aubrey were no secret to him (or anyone else at CBS), his letter to her smacks of gallantry and a desire to afford her some public face-saving. His private opinion of Judy, however, was widely circulated throughout Television City.

Chapter 10

I was out of a job and a marriage. The job had been a disturbing and sometimes fascinating experience. The marriage qualified as a blood brother to the job, the only difference being it had dragged on for years instead of months. There is a standard Father-speech, a statement that ranks in wisdom alongside Polonius's advice to his son, a dictum directed toward a marriage-minded male offspring. "Wait," it begins. "Just wait. Right now, she's all sweetness, she's all charm, whatever you want to do she wants to do, she's the perfect girl. But the minute you put that ring on her finger, watch what happens. An amazing change takes place. All of a sudden, these interests of yours will, overnight, be boring to her. All of a sudden she'll want to pick out your clothes, tell you what to eat, how to talk and you'll go, not where *you* want to go, but where *she* wants to go.

Believe me, I know! Haven't I been married to your mother for a hundred years?"

There was no "amazing change" in Snow White after we were married. From the moment I met her, I was well aware of her volatile personality, her stubborn determination (once, when she felt she was being overcharged for an item in a Walgreen's drugstore in Dallas, she spent the best part of two hours on the long-distance telephone until she got through to the *president* of the company and berated him mercilessly for the sixty-five-cent discrepancy in the price of a pair of nylons!), and most of all, her obsession with the continuing premise that she had to win at all costs in everything she undertook. This last trait made game playing of any sort a contest of wills as opposed to a period of recreation.

She was also a very beautiful girl, an item which was not exactly a deterrent in my desire to marry her. I was certain some of her less attractive characteristics would dissolve like aspirin once I made an "honest woman" of her. That was a mistake I would live to regret.

It is tempting to indulge in self-vindication, but I would be far from honest if I did not present both sides of the coin. Any woman who becomes implicated in a marriage to an actor, singer or comic usually finds herself saddled with a complex, self-centered, absent-minded, preoccupied, frequently tactless individual who, more often than not, needs constant care, feeding and ego building. Show business is like no business I know. So much is left to timing, chance, luck, fate, who and not what you know, with talent so often being the tiniest ingredient in the bouillabaisse, that the very nature of the beast, the fragile quality of success, makes for insecurity, ulcers, depression on a grand scale and not infrequent heart attacks.

It is pointless to beat one's breast about it. That's the way it is, and nobody forces you to play in the game. I am merely pointing out simple truths that exist, not only in the entertainment business but in every line of work in a competitive world, although I do believe that show business does foster and nurture more unqualified people than does any other supposedly skilled profession.

Perhaps Snow White was unaware of these tribulations when we met. She certainly was pitched headlong into a nightmare of constant traveling, irregular periods of dining and general turmoil that went against her grain and was as grating on her nerves as a piece of chalk on a blackboard. Still, she was well aware of what I did, and it was never a secret to her that "the road" made up the greater part of my income.

All of the foregoing is, of course, superfluous. Two weeks after I was fired from the Garland show, certain irrefutable facts came to my attention that precluded the possibility of continuing the marriage. Ahead lay a long, drawn-out period of waiting; waiting to go to court for temporary separation, waiting for a year just to have the case come up on the overcrowded Los Angeles divorce docket and then another yearlong wait before the decree was final. I had followed Shribman's advice and stayed in town until the final Garland show had been taped. Now I wanted to be somewhere else, anywhere, away from the ignominy of failure at both my marriage and my recent employment. Where could I escape to?

"Well," said Joe Shribman, "we got an offer here that you've been turning down for two years." He mentioned a club in San Jose, California.

"I'll take it."

"You're kidding?"

"Like hell I am. I'll take it."

"Don't you even want to know the money?"

"Is it over scale?"

He laughed. "Jesus, you do want to get away, don't you?"

"How soon can I leave?"

"Let's see," he said, referring to a booking notebook on his desk. "You could open Friday, that's three days from now."

"Call them and confirm it, will you?"

"You realize it's for two weeks."

"The way I'm feeling right now, I wish it were for two months!"

"Bad as that?"

"Worse."

"Want me to make plane reservations? Oh, and where do you want to stay? The club's not in the center of town, you know. It's in the suburbs."

"The suburbs?" I laughed. "*San Jose* is the suburbs."

"Their chamber of commerce won't like you."

"I think I'll drive up in the Corvette. Find me a good, modern motel somewhere near the club, would you please?"

"Sure. Anything I can do?" He asked me if I would like him to talk to my wife.

"No, Joseph, leave it alone. It's all over, and it's going to stay that way."

I told him I would not be averse to continuing on from San Jose and asked him to put together some kind of tour, wherever it might lead. Then I thanked him and headed for the house.

Although I was not to leave for a few days, I felt it wise

to move out immediately. As I packed, there followed a bar-
rage of recriminations, denials, threats, entreaties; but I was
resolute. The time for going had come. I walked back into
Tracy's bedroom to say good-by. He sat on the floor, playing with a toy car, and when I lifted him into my arms, his
bewildered anxiety over the household situation that he
could not, of course, understand but that he deeply sensed,
nearly overcame my firm resolve. I fought the urge to weep
as he asked the time-worn questions: "Where are you going,
Daddy?" "When will you be back?" And that fine old chest-
nut, "Don't you love Mommy and me anymore?" As I held
him, I realized just how much I did love him and that I had
neglected him shamefully during the past nine months. Two
young Mexican girls had come to live in the house months
before, and Tracy had, almost exclusively, been their responsibility. Now, the temptation to remain in the house
and personally direct his upbringing was all but irresistible.
On the other hand the pretense of a continuing relationship
between his mother and myself might, in the end, produce
far-reaching negative results and mental scars that he would
find much more difficult to surmount in later life.

I put him down, kissed him and spoke a few soothing
words of farewell, with the promise I would see him soon
and call him on the phone from where I was going. Like my
recent motorcycle accident, when I had had the sense to
realize the importance of getting back on the bike, then and
there, despite every smarting fiber of my body crying out
against it, I knew if I did not leave instantly, I might not
ever go, and the course of my life, Tracy's and Snow White's
would be altered for the worse. The day was overcast and
gloomy, and the last thing I recall as I pulled away from the
house was Tracy watching me leave, standing in the large

window to the left of the front door, sad-eyed, clutching his toy car to his chest like a substitute security blanket.

I called Frank and John to say good-by.

"San Jose?" yelled Frank over the phone. "My God, that's where the elephants go to die!"

"Oh well, Captain, it won't be so sad. I'll have my books, my music and my memories."

"And where from there?" asked John.

"Wherever Shribman, GAC (my agents) and God deign to send me."

"Anything new on your money from Garland?" asked Frank.

"No, but my lawyer's on top of it. It's safe and sound, at least. Judy can't touch it and neither can I. I guess it'll all be straightened away before very long."

"Hey, keep in touch, will you?" said Frank.

"I will."

"No, we mean it, guy. Let us hear from you, 'cause if we don't, we'll track you down and chew you out."

"Yeah," echoed John. "Forewarned is forearmed. Remember that, Number One!"

"I will, Binky. I will."

Early Thursday evening, I headed for San Jose.

It was raining heavily as I drove through the night, and my elbow was bothering me. The healing process had been slower than I had imagined it would be, and, as with many forms of injuries, wet weather would affect the arm for the rest of my life. The car was warm, though, with the radio playing softly and an overall feeling of coziness pervaded the Corvette cockpit. I sped toward northern California, fighting the hypnotic sweep of the wipers on the windshield, favoring my aching elbow, as I indulged in some deep thinking.

What was going to happen to my little boy? How would he turn out? One of the most repeated phrases heard in connection with divorce is: "Don't worry about the kid(s). Kids are tough. They survive."

True enough, perhaps, but does the end, survival, justify the means? Is it enough to allow a child to fend for himself or is a father derelict in his love and duty unless he takes positive action toward a constructive, loving, educational program where his child is concerned? I would have to meditate on Tracy's future well-being.

I checked into the Hyatt House Motor Hotel, just off Highway 101, south of San Jose, in the early-morning hours. I was bone-weary, and driving rain lulled me into a dreamless sleep. I was awakened late the following morning by a sound that my subconscious mind catalogued as a lawnmower motor. I opened my eyes, stretched, walked to the window and opened the curtain. The rain had given way to a beautiful morning, sparkling, still, with a clear blue sky and bright sunlight. As I gazed out the window, my "lawn mower" came to life, sprouted wings and lifted off the ground before my eyes. The motor noises my sleep-fogged mind had incorrectly identified were actually the sounds of airplane engines emanating from San Jose Muncipal Airport, a mere spitting distance from the motel.

Light plane after light plane was taking off into the windless morning and the cloudless skies. Cessnas, Pipers, Bonanzas, intermittent airliners, all were being drawn into the air as if by some invisible sky hook. It was a tableau of grace and beauty, and I wished at that moment I were part of it instead of a groundling observer. I looked at my watch on the nightstand. My rehearsal at the club was not until four in the afternoon. The best part of the day was mine for the taking.

I got into some sports clothes, had breakfast and slowly drove over to the adjacent airport. I parked the car near a small building that bore the legend: "San Jose Piper Sales." Somehow, I found myself inside the little structure, where an affable man greeted me, introducing himself as the owner and manager of the establishment and asking what he could do for me.

When I mumbled something about having seen the planes from my motel window and wanting to get a look at them up close, he smiled in understanding.

"You're Mel Tormé, aren't you?"

"Yes, that's right."

"I saw where you were opening at the Safari tonight. My wife and I plan to come and see you."

"Thank you. I hope you'll enjoy the show."

"You like airplanes, huh?"

"I sure do. Always have."

"You a pilot?"

"No, 'fraid not. I like airplanes but I hate flying."

"Really? Why? Have you ever tried it? Private flying, I mean."

"Yes. Once."

I remembered my first and only experience in a light plane. It had been during the war. David Street, a singer and musician I had known, invited me to "take a ride" in his light plane. We drove out to Clover Field (now Santa Monica Municipal Airport). It was little more than a cinder strip in those days, a sparsely used airport with somewhat limited facilities. We climbed into his plane, a tiny Luscombe Silvaire 85, and took off. I was enjoying the flight immensely, when, without warning, at around five thousand feet over Malibu, David said casually, "I'm going to do a spin." Suddenly the nose lifted until a stall was accomplished, then it fell off on one wing and proceeded to spin earthward. That was the single most frightening experience of my life. There was no reference point with which to identify, total loss of a sense of balance, with positive G forces jamming me deeply into my seat, and in that insane, whirling, blurry world of motion, I felt trapped, and worse, doomed. When he neutralized the controls, added power and once again regained straight and level flight, I wanted out, quickly and badly.

From that moment on, a deep fear of light aircraft was instilled in me.

Another man entered the sales office. He was a big, square-built guy with a cleanly shaven dome, who was introduced to me as Duane Allen, chief flying instructor for San Jose Piper Sales.

"Want to do a little flying?" he asked with a friendly grin.

"I—uh—no, I don't think so, thank you. I just came over to—watch."

"Not as good as the real thing."

"Go ahead, Mel," said the owner of the place. "There's a little Cherokee 140 just outside that we use for student instruction. Why not take a ride with Duane? You look like a born pilot to me."

I grinned ruefully. "If you only knew."

Duane's eyes narrowed slightly. "Bad experience in an airplane?"

"Bingo!" I said. "Real bad, Duane. I'm ashamed to admit it left me a permanent groundhog."

"Nonsense!" he snapped. "There's absolutely nothing to be afraid of. Come on, I'll show you."

I looked at him reluctantly. "Well, all right," I agreed. "But no spins!"

"Spins?" he roared. "Who the hell does spins in a Piper Cherokee?"

"Well," I said nervously, "I just don't think I want———"

"Look," he explained patiently, "these airplanes aren't rated for aerobatics, see? I couldn't and wouldn't do a spin in one if I wanted to."

And that, dear reader, is how someone as unlikely as I became a pilot!

On that first afternoon I took not one, but two lessons in the gentle art of aviating. The first hour, the "white knuckle" flight, was spent making friends with that complex beast, the Cherokee 140, a machine that seemed terrifyingly incomprehensible, inherently unstable, prone to violent attacks of yaw and roll and pitch. The whole lesson was spent with a death grip on the yoke (control wheel), playing a highly advanced game of rubbing-my-stomach-patting-my-head.

After we landed and my heart left my mouth and found its way back to my chest, we tried again. The second time up, things began to sort themselves out. Duane tolerantly explained this was an aircraft, not a Mack truck, and that very little pressure need be applied to the controls in order to make it sit up and beg. By the end of that second hour of instruction, I was amazed to find I could do reasonable power-off stalls, raise and lower the nose and turn the Cherokee to the right or the left without skidding around all over the sky. My landing attempts were way too high, and every time I flared out over the runway, we would drop like a stone and slam down on the strip. I looked at Duane apprehensively.

"Relax," he grinned. "This baby is built to take it. She's not about to come apart on you." By midafternoon I had even made an acceptable landing (which is to say, we both walked away from it without serious injury). Before I left the airport that afternoon, I signed up for the full treatment, and as I got in the car, I shot a quick, affectionate look at the little red-and-white Cherokee, parked on the tarmac. Far from the unconquerable monster I had imagined her to be, I suddenly knew she was a permissive, forgiving mistress and that we would get to know each other very well.

For the next two weeks I was plunged into the absorbing world of ground school: meteorology, flying theory, proper use of the two-way radio, navigation by map reading and radio-navigational aids, plus instruction in the manipulation of a computer which, when implemented correctly, gives you readings on fuel consumption, ground speed, true air speed, wind adjustments and countless other computations designed to bedazzle the brain and keep you awake nights.

The people with whom I associated during that period were among the finest I have ever known. Flying enthusiasts are truly a breed apart, with the special sense of sharing that is indigenous to the aviation world. There is a delightful lack of selfishness among pilots. The one universal desire seems to be to help fellow birdmen become proficient in the art of handling a plane. Toward this end, almost every single flier I have met has given up his own valuable time and recreation to help someone less knowledgeable or experienced over the hurdles of the written exam (which is tough), or the nerve-wracking flight check that springboards a student pilot into private-pilot status.

I was staying in close touch with my lawyer, who was not only handling the Garland matter but my divorce proceeding as well. Judy had reportedly raised hell when she found I had tied up all that money, and my wife was equally irate for other reasons. The concentrated effort I was making as a novice flier was also serving to clear my head and help me evaluate Tracy's future welfare. Eight days after I arrived in San Jose, I made up my mind to seek custody of my son. I had decided he would be far better off with me, and I made a personal vow to devote a great deal of time, effort and money toward his education, care and character development. I was not deluding myself. Custody to the father in California is rare, particularly to a man who travels extensively. I was determined to try to get Tracy if I could, but if the judge decided it would not be in his best interests to stay with me, then I would swallow my medicine and learn to live with the next best thing: visitation.

I pondered this decision on my ninth day in northern California, at thirty-five hundred feet above sea level. Duane and I had taken off from San Jose Municipal, made a right turn and climbed out over the hills to practice. Updraughts and downdraughts, which are common to hilly areas, caught us and bounced the little Cherokee, but thanks to Duane's clinical explanation of this condition, I had lost my lifelong fear of turbulence. Now, as we bumped our way over the low mountains, he sat in the right seat, grinning like a barrel-chested Tartar. "You don't really know you're flying unless it's a little bumpy," he chortled happily. I was able to grin back. I had changed in the past week and a half. I was not fretting over my problems to any great extent. Sitting in the left seat of an airplane, in charge of the controls, was wonderfully unrelated to show business. I was even feeling a little cocky. Had I really been afraid of airplanes less than two weeks ago? Hard to believe. Here I was, relaxed, comfortable, taking to flying like a duck to water.

We practiced "S" turns, stalls and Omni-navigation, the art of flying from point to point by means of a 360° VHF radio beam that corresponds to a numbered setting on a cockpit instrument and guides you unerringly to your destination. After an hour and a half of practice, we landed and taxied toward the parking stand. As we pulled up, Duane cautioned, "Don't kill the engine." He opened the door, climbed out and said, supercasually, "Okay. Take her around the pattern once by yourself."

At first I could not believe my ears. I was ready to solo, at least as far as Duane was concerned. Suddenly, I wasn't so cocky. Me fly an airplane *all alone?* With that chilling thought came another, almost simultaneously; I *am* ready. Without another word, I closed the door, taxied back to the run-up line, checked my instruments and controls, ran the engine up to 1800 rpm's, tested both magnetos and called the tower: "San Jose tower, this is Cherokee seven-five-seven-zero Whiskey ready to go on three-zero right."

"Cherokee seven-zero Whiskey, clear to take off."

Slowly I applied pressure to the hand throttle, and the airplane crept forward on the runway, gaining speed as she rolled. At sixty miles an hour I rotated, applying back pressure on the yoke. The Cherokee (this one a 180-horsepower model), left the ground and climbed swiftly. As soon as I had cleared the active, I made a climbing right-hand turn and proceeded at pattern altitude (800 feet above the runway) to execute a good, square pattern of my own, turning right again into the downwind leg, perfectly parallel with the runway, calling the tower to inform them I was going to land. Then, past the entry point of three-one right, another right turn, the base leg of the landing sequence, losing altitude slowly, decreasing the power, applying one notch of flap to further slow the airplane down and steepen the angle of descent. Well lined up now, the final right turn was made, and there was the runway, floating up to meet me. As soon as I crossed the giant white numbers that proclaim the magnetic compass heading of every airport runway, I gently eased the wheel back into my stomach. It was the best landing I have ever made.

I was jubilant that afternoon as I thanked Duane and his colleagues for their patience and encouragement. Being a self-taught musician-arranger, I had been dubious about my ability to absorb and understand anything technical on an instructive, academic level. As I drove away that day, I felt a greater sense of accomplishment than I had ever known before. Since it was still early afternoon, I decided to go into San Jose and see a movie. I parked in town, bought a paper and there, in the amusement section, staring at me from a large ad, was The Legend, appearing in a rerun of *A Star Is Born*. I can't escape, I thought lightly, and decided, since I felt so good that nothing could depress me, I would go and see it again.

I had forgotten the power of Judy's performance in that film. The sequence in which she returns to her home from the studio and does a wild, exciting number, jumping up and down on all the furniture in an effort to cheer up her faded-movie-star husband, could hardly have been better, and the dressing-room scene in which she cries out her despair over his drinking and his mental demoralization rates among the finest acting performances ever filmed.

I left the theater more convinced than ever of her enor-

mous ability as an actress and a performer. I would be happy
when this nasty business of the lawsuit was finished. I was
experiencing some misgivings over it, but I was in no position to be impractical. My lawyer had warned me only
yesterday that a custody suit was lengthy and expensive. I
would need the Garland money, and a lot more before it was
all over.

An engagement in San Francisco followed the San Jose
date, and I was able to continue my flying lessons with
Duane, who would bring a Cherokee over to Oakland airport daily, where I would meet him and press on. That was
a relatively happy time. Even the near-daily phone calls
from Snow White could not diminish the enjoyment of this
learning time. Her frequent diatribes were filled with more
rancor than usual now that she had been informed of my
intention to fight for Tracy. To respond in kind would have
been a waste of time, but on one or two occasions, my temper got the better of me and the long-distance telephone
lines must have burned to a crisp.

I headed East now, playing a few clubs, doing a concert
or two, appearing on this TV game show or that late-night
talk show in New York. Shribman had arranged a two-week
stand at the Crystal Theater of the famous Tivoli Gardens
in Copenhagen and then a few TV appearances in London,
a city that he knew ranked as my favorite in the world.

The Danes were extremely kind to me, personally and
professionally. I rented a motor-scooter and saw much of
the beautiful Scandinavian countryside in the weeks I spent
there. London, that summer, was full of movie folk, among
them Stu Whitman, busy making *Those Magnificent Men
in Their Flying Machines,* and a fellow aviation enthusiast,

Cliff Robertson, who had been taking lessons for weeks at a small flying field in Surrey, just outside London.

On the evening of July 4, Cliff and I headed for Fair Oaks aerodrome, where a couple of RAF types took us aloft in a pair of Tiger Moths for an exciting tailchase. It was my first experience in an open-cockpit biplane, and I enjoyed it tremendously. Cliff soloed later on that evening in one of the Moths. The summer sun was still strong at nine in the evening as he took off from the broad green field and made his solo circuit, while I took pictures of the event with a 16mm camera.

One week later, in Newcastle-upon-Tyne, where I was appearing for a six-day stand, I rented a Tiger Moth and took several hours of dual instruction. It was such a comfortable ship to fly that I actually learned to spin it! I left England shortly afterward and flew home on a big jet, convinced that air travel was the only way to go. Midway across the Atlantic, we ran into a large storm, replete with blinding flashes of lightning and extreme turbulence. During the hour or so in which we were tossed, bumped and lashed like a matchstick in the wind, my convictions about traveling by air diminished considerably. In fact they dwindled into the realm of the minuscule, and in addition to incanting several prayers, a single sentence kept flashing its way across my eyes, like the moving sign on the Times Square Building: "If God had meant Man to fly . . ." You know the rest.

In August, I went to court and won temporary custody of Tracy. I took him to Hawaii with me, and, for the first time in over a year, we got to know each other. When I brought him back to California in time for the fall school term, we had established a relationship that was to grow in love and respect.

My lawyer asked for a meeting to determine whether or not we should try to settle my claim against Judy out of court. GAC and Joe Shribman voted against that course of action, pointing out that the money was safe enough in the CBS coffers and that the prospect of my receiving the full amount was excellent.

With that reassuring thought in mind, I headed East for a few weeks in order to stockpile dollars in anticipation of the forthcoming court battle. With the court's approval, my mother and father took charge of Tracy for this period.

Late in September, Duane Allen, flying a Piper Cherokee 235, met me in Niagara Falls, New York. With Duane in the right seat to keep me from doing anything dumb, we took off in the early dawn on September 21 and headed for California. Three days later, having flown across the country through every conceivable kind of weather, we landed at Santa Monica Municipal Airport. As I taxied toward a parking tie-down, I looked around and remembered my first light-plane ride with Dave Street from this broad, paved runway, which at that time had seemed more like a short, cindery country lane. That day, I had vowed I would never ride in one of the little "puddle jumpers" again. Now, some eighteen years later, I had flown one the width of the nation. Incredible, I thought, what a little orientation will accomplish.

I resisted many tempting offers of work for the next couple of months. I wanted to spend Christmas with Tracy, in the little house I had rented. My mother and father had moved in to help take care of him, and though it was not nearly so posh as my previous manse had been, I found it warm and, most important, homelike. Trace was getting on well in school. I got into a routine of dropping him off there every morning, then heading for Santa Monica Municipal for early A.M. practice in a Cherokee.

One Christmas present I was unprepared for was a disturbing call from my lawyer. He informed me the Internal Revenue Service, in a swift move to collect some of the taxes for which Garland was in arrears, had swooped down on CBS and confiscated the money they had been holding in escrow for me. It was a real blow. I argued vainly that it had been my understanding the money was inviolate, untouchable; but I was quickly corrected. The government, I was informed, takes precedent over everything. Forget that money. It is gone. What happens now, I asked, dejectedly. We fight, was the answer. We take Garland to court, and we fight. We'll have to requisition her personal-appearance earnings. What about Judy? Where was she? Was she working again? Yes, she was doing some concerts, the whereabouts of which were somewhat vaguely reported. Did she go on that tour of the Orient? Don't know, was the reply.

From other sources I found out she had broken with Bobby Cole soon after the show had terminated. It was presumed he had gone back to New York. The various members of the Garland staff were all involved in new ventures, and the recent madness was little more than a memory. Defunct television series, like the pain of a dentist's drill, are quickly forgotten once you are away from them.

I spent a quiet New Year's Eve at home, but funds were getting low. In February, I was offered a two-week engagement at an exclusive new club in London, the Cool Elephant, and I accepted. During my stay there, I met and fell in love with an English actress, whom I had admired in films for some time. Though it was not the most propitious time for a love affair, I knew instinctively that if I rejected involvement with this extraordinary young woman, I would kick myself for the rest of my life.

In early April I went to New York to appear on the Sammy Davis television show. On the day of taping, Sammy and I did a duet, after which there was to be a scene change. While we were waiting he grabbed my arm and led me toward a front-row spectator, Judy Garland. It was the first time we had seen each other since that night she had embarrassed me in front of the band and I had gone up to my office and packed.

"Hi, honey," she said tentatively, a half-smile on her face.

"Well, hello."

"That was a great number you and Sammy did. Did you arrange it?"

"Uh-huh."

"Well, it was great. Just great."

"Thanks. How are you? How are the kids?"

"Oh, they're fine, just fine. They're back in L.A. In school."

"What are you doing in town? You working?"

"No. No, just playing. You know me and New York. I love it." She looked good, smartly dressed and fairly happy, if surface appearances were any criteria. I was being called to start the next number. Impulsively, I took her hand and kissed it.

"Good to see you, Jude."

"You too," she smiled. "Take care."

The next time we met, the occasion was somewhat more formal. It was a few weeks later, in the conference room of my lawyer's suite of offices. She had been summoned to give a deposition, and I was requested to be present. She arrived fifteen minutes late, flanked by her own attorneys.

She wore a dark suit, trimmed in fur, and a preposterous little hat to match. Her face seemed slightly puffy and her eyes looked sunken. I had no doubt she had dreaded this meeting, and, at that moment, a disturbing thought crossed my mind. For the first time since I had met her, she did look like "a little old lady." I found that very sad.

"Hello, Sadie," I said gently.

She smiled wanly. "I told you before, and I'll tell you again," she said, shaking her head slowly from side to side. "Don't call me Sadie."

We got to the business at hand very quickly.

The taking of a deposition can be, for the most part, a dull, deadly affair. Boring vital statistics (such as the fine points in the drawing up of contracts, the establishing of dates, places, etc.) are discussed over and over again. Consequently, in the interests of readability and practicality, what follows are the most pertinent excerpts from the Judy Garland deposition.

Judy was represented on this occasion by her attorney, Mr. Schwab, as well as a man she introduced as Mr. Brent. My attorney's name was Daniel Sklar. (Note: "Q" indicates Mr. Sklar's questions; "A," Miss Garland's replies.)

After fully twenty minutes of general questioning, Sklar got to the specifics:

> Q Did there come a time when Mr. Tormé's services on the Judy Garland Show were terminated?
> A Yes.
> Q At whose instructions were his services terminated?
> A Mine.
> Q To whom did you give this instruction?

A   To the producer who was then Bill Colleran.

Q   What exactly did you tell Mr. Colleran at that time?

A   That Mr. Tormé had not appeared to do his job, and I couldn't pay him any more.

Q   What did Mr. Colleran say?

A   He said, "You are right."

Q   And you told him to take the necessary steps to terminate?

A   No, no. Yes, I did. I did. He was the producer. I didn't go much further than that. I had to get another musical arranger, you see.

Q   Did you pay another musical arranger?

A   I had to.

Q   Did you?

A   Yes.

Q   Who did you obtain?

A   Bobby Cole, who was originally just supposed to do one guest appearance.

Q   When did you engage Mr. Cole?

A   I don't know, Mr. Sklar. I really don't. I think it was in February some time.

Q   Was this before or after the Jack Jones show which you referred to?

A   It was before. It was just before, just before the Jack Jones show, but he was only hired to appear.

Q   When did you hire him as the vocal arranger?

A   I just told you—oh, no—after Mr. Tormé left the show.

Q   That is what I am asking, about him not as a performer, but as the vocal arranger for the show?

A   Yes, somebody had to do the arrangements.

Q   You engaged him after?

A   After Mr. Tormé left.

Q   After you gave, after you told Mr. Colleran?

A   No, I didn't tell. Mel walked out.

Q   Let's then go back.

A   And I didn't have any recourse except to get somebody to arrange for the future guest appearances of the guest stars.

Q   You say Mr. Tormé walked out?

A   Yes.

Q   When did he walk out?

A   He walked out in the middle of the Jack Jones show. He wrote the songs. He wrote the arrangements. They were very difficult to learn, the duets, but then he wouldn't appear to conduct and cue us or teach us the notes and songs.

Q   Had you had a discussion with Mr. Tormé prior to the Jack Jones show?

A   No, sir. I was very surprised.

Q   You say he walked out. By that you mean that he was not present?

A   He wasn't present.

Q   At what time did you first notice that he was not present?

A   In the middle of the Jack Jones show, when we were supposed to learn his arrangements. He wasn't there to teach it.

Q   Was this before the taping, or the prerecording?

A   Before the taping.

Q   Before the pre-recording?

A   The pre-recording and taping was done at the

same time on that show. There was no pre-recording on that show. It was done live.

Q   It was done live?

A   Yes.

Q   That would be done on a Friday?

A   We usually did them on Friday, yes.

Q   Was this particular show done on a Friday?

A   Yes.

Q   When did you notice for the first time that Mr. Tormé was not present?

A   I think about 3:00 o'clock in the afternoon.

Q   On that Friday?

A   Yes.

Q   Did you inquire as to where he was?

A   Yes.

Q   Who did you inquire of?

A   I tried to reach Mr. Tormé myself on the telephone.

Q   How did you try to reach him?

A   I called his house. He wouldn't answer the phone.
    I tried to reach him through the producer, through CBS, and he could not be reached. He would not come to the phone.

Q   And you had had no previous discussions with him?

A   No.

Q   You had had no previous discussion with him with respect to his being there on that Friday?

A   No, I did not.

Q   In this Jack Jones show, was the material written by Mr. Tormé?

A   Yes. It was very difficult. It was written by Mr. Tormé. That was used, but we had to learn it from the pianist in the band, because neither Jack Jones nor I can read music, so it is kind of touch-and-go.

MR. SCHWAB: I make a motion to strike that. That is a volunteered statement of the witness.

(After eight more pages of repetitious questions and answers, Mr. Sklar brought this line of questioning to a close.)

Q So if I can get the sequence in mind, you did the Jack Jones show on February 21, and then you observed that Mr. Tormé was not there and you were unable to locate him?

A Yes.

BY MR. SKLAR: . . . (So,) you asked Mr. Colleran to terminate Mr. Tormé's services?

A I asked CBS and Mr. Colleran.

Q Who did you ask?

A And Kingsrow, myself, because I can't pay people who don't work.

(At this point, Judy asked for a brief recess while she got a glass of water and repaired to the powder room. The questioning had tired her. When she returned to the conference room, and the taking of the deposition was resumed, she seemed far less aggressive and more inclined toward accuracy than before.)

Q Did there come a time at or about, prior to the Jack Jones show, when you made a decision to do the remaining programs of the Judy Garland Show as concert shows?

THE WITNESS: I made a decision because I could only do 26 shows. Mr. Tormé had appeared on four already, and I had to do concert form, and I had to resign. I discussed this with Mr.

Tormé prior to the Jack Jones show, and
he seemed amenable. He seemed a little
upset, but finally said, "All right. I understand." So that is the last I remember, that he
just——

Q   When you say you discussed it with Mr.
    Tormé, what was it that you discussed with
    him?

A   His not appearing for the final two shows to
    make up for the six.

Q   In other words, you advised him that——

A   —that I had to do concert form.

Q   That you were going to do concert form, and
    he would not appear?

A   I tried to explain that he had appeared four
    times, and I thought it would be wiser for the
    show as long as I had to resign, that it was
    quite friendly.
    Mel said he understood. He had already ap-
    peared four times, and that was the end of
    that.

Q   And you advised or discussed with Mr. Tormé
    the fact that your plan for the remaining
    shows did not include having him appear on
    one of those concert shows?

A   I didn't think it would be wise, because it
    wasn't financially right, and it wasn't correct
    from a showmanship point of view.

Q   By "financially correct," what did you mean?

A   When you do a show in concert form and you
    just sing and don't—you don't have to hire
    lots of writers for dialogue, that is what I
    wanted to do all along anyway, so it was

much less expensive. I think it was something like $10,000 less, or something.

Q In other words, that decision involved the fact that you would not need writers to write dialogue for you?

A No. It affected the discussion between Mr. Tormé and myself, it had to do with the fact that he had appeared four times, and I only had four more shows to go, and I didn't think it was wise for Mr. Tormé or the show to appear two more times.

Q And you conveyed that thought to Mr. Tormé?

A Yes.

Q Did you discuss also with him whether you would require him to continue to write?

A Oh, yes, yes.

Q The shows?

A Oh, yes, yes.

Q So that you discussed with him the fact that he could continue to arrange music?

A Oh, yes, indeed.

Q But he would not appear at any of the next remaining shows?

A That is right. We discussed it, and he seemed to, he seemed a bit disappointed at first, but then he understood, but I never advised him not to supervise——

Q ——the music?

A ——the music.

Q Did you advise him that he would be paid for those two appearances, even though he didn't do the——

A I don't know. I don't really know. I imagine

that would come under the contractual—I really don't know, did we discuss that aspect or not. I will say this: I expected him to continue performing as supervisor of music.

Q Did Mr. Cole do any of the writing for the Jack Jones show?

A No, Mr. Tormé did that, but he wasn't there to teach us the notes and the arrangements and to conduct.

Q But he did the writing?

A He did the writing.

Q And he did the arrangements?

A Yes.

Q In other words, he did the arrangements and the writing of the music and delivered them to the orchestra, or Mort Lindsey, I would suppose?

A Yes.

Q And so he did that part of his work?

A Yes.

Q But he was not there as you say, to conduct?

A Yes, which was very necessary——

Q —for the rehearsal?

A Yes.

Q These musical arrangements and so on for the Jack Jones show were prepared by Mr. Tormé and delivered to the orchestra?

A Yes.

MR. SKLAR: That is all.

It had been arduous for her. Now, she took a deep breath, got up and asked to use the powder room again. Her attorneys took this opportunity to check in with their respective offices, and my lawyer went back into his personal office to answer a few calls that had come in during the taking of the deposition.

I was left alone in the conference room to consider what I had just heard. The wonder of it was that Judy, after the passing of time, had seemingly come to believe what she was saying. The "squeeze play" she had perpetrated during those last weeks of the show, her calculated rudeness to me in an effort to force my resignation, all of it was conveniently forgotten, homogenized into the whole milk, and what now prevailed within her was a mental state of righteous indignation and self-justification.

I could not tell whether or not she had rehearsed her reactions and responses, whether her attorneys had put her through a rigorous coaching course just prior to her arrival at my lawyer's lair. It was always wise to keep in mind her inestimable acting ability. I was inclined, on the other hand, to subscribe to my first reaction; she now actually believed the events in question as having taken place exactly as she had described them, completely vindicating her judgment in firing me and withholding monies *I claimed* she owed me.

It was senseless to be angry with her, unthinkable to hate her. She looked indescribably weary at the end of the questioning, Earth-mother with the weight of the universe on her tiny shoulders.

And what the hell, she *was* Judy Garland. I found it difficult to keep from remembering that. She was an institution, like the Smithsonian, or the National Gallery, like Social Security and income tax. I had grown up with her, hunkered in my seat on Saturday afternoons at the Shore Theater on Chicago's south side, while up there, on the screen, she and Mickey had held hands and sung about "Our Love Affair." I remembered her now in *Pigskin Pa-*

rade, fresh and young, eyes shining, as she stood up in the grandstand and cheered the football hero on to victory with "It's Love I'm After." I recalled the drab, sepia-toned vastness of the Kansas prairie she called "home" in *The Wizard of Oz,* her heart-rending pleas to Aunt Em to save Toto from the clutches of an unrelenting Margaret Hamilton, and the eye-appealing contrast of Oz, splendid in the muted Technicolor tones of the thirties that were so much more true-to-life than today's garish processes.

I thought of that first time I had seen her, at Donald O'Connor's shindig back in the forties, and realized she looked as wistful and vulnerable today as she had on that evening, over twenty years before.

Then there were her unsuccessful marriages and numerous romances. She needed love and understanding. She craved it more than anything else in the world, or so I believed. Yet every relationship had failed. Why? Some of it, perhaps most of it, was her own fault. Still, was she *responsible?* Was she actively, knowingly difficult, or was it part of her overall psyche, a throwback to her unhappy days at Metro? Was she striking back at life blindfolded, getting even for former abuses, not really caring who got in the way?

Even with her personal problems, her well-known addiction to "Wake-me-up-now-put-me-to-sleep-now-calm-me-down" pills, her unpredictable behavior with concert promotors, showing up hours late and, reportedly, not at all on a few occasions, she was undisputedly a one-of-a-kind human being and artist. No one could deny this. She had played the *enfant terrible* over and over throughout her stormy career. Yet prominent, talented people from virtually every walk of life idolized her, swore by her, defended and protected her, a combined show of fealty unrivaled in the business.

I could not help dwelling for a moment on her kindness to me that evening when she and Sinatra had come to see me at the Crescendo, and then my thoughts turned to "The Judy Garland Show" itself. It had been agonizing, at times downright infuriating. It had also been great fun on occasion. I recalled the Ol' Blue jacket emblems; how I had been set up by Judy when I had asked her to sing "Buds Won't Bud," how perfectly she had uttered that four-letter word so repugnant to me, to everyone's (including my own) amusement; of her insistence that I remain when Team No. 1 was dismissed; I remembered my birthday and the ill-fated cake and the laughter of the audience when it spread its frosty creaminess all over the stage; the Christmas party at Matteo's, and the carols she and I had sung together.

And there were other great moments. Her first, emotion-packed rendition of "The Battle Hymn," her superb one-upmanship that day in the rehearsal hall vis-à-vis Barbra Streisand, the unfailing, tear-inducing experience when she sang "Over the Rainbow" on the Christmas show. I tried now to weigh the good against the bad, the uplifting versus the downgrading. The Dawn Patrol, the tantrums, the deviousness, the unprofessionalism, even the lies she had told during the deposition-taking, conscious or not, seemed to pale beside the overall value of my nine-month association with her. I found myself feeling like the rat fink of all time. That I was in the right was after the fact. I was suing Judy Garland, and so was just about everyone else. Daily, the papers told of new litigations brought against her for unpaid bills, back taxes and the like. How, in God's name, I wondered, could anyone survive such an onslaught of seemingly insurmountable financial problems?

Could she ever pull herself together long enough to earn the king's ransom it would take to pay all her debtors? Christ, I thought suddenly, what's going to happen to Judy Garland? And as simply and quickly as that, I knew I could not go through with the lawsuit.

When I told my lawyer, he stared at me in disbelief.

"Do you know how much this deposition is going to cost?"

"No. I suppose it will be expensive, but——"

"It's throwing good money after bad, Mel. Why the change of heart?"

"I don't know. I—all of a sudden I just lost interest in suing the poor dame. She's got enough troubles."

"You've got troubles too, or have you forgotten? Getting permanent custody of your son—and remember, there's no guarantee we'll be successful—is going to drain you financially, you know that. Between court costs, attorney's fees, back taxes, division of community property and what-have-you, you're going to have to start all over again. Now, in my considered opinion, this is one hell of a time for an attack of altruism where Judy Garland is concerned."

"There's nothing altruistic about this decision, Dan. Let's just say I feel the money's uncollectable. I've got a—I don't know—call it a premonition, that she's not going to bounce back this time. She seems sort of resigned, know what I mean? I'll bet even if she does some concerts, or a few movies, the government will step right in and grab the money before she knows what's happened."

"All right. You'd win that bet, but——"

"Look, I know what we're facing in the divorce. And I'm

as concerned as you about the financial end. But, thank God, I know where I'm going. I can recoup and rebuild my bank account. Judy? I think she's lost. I have a feeling this is one time she's not going to rise from the ashes and, don't laugh, seeing her today, looking like she does, even when she bent the truth to fit her own interests, I felt damn sorry for her."

I took a deep breath and said, "Let's leave it, Dan. No matter how many problems I have right now, I'm in a lot better shape than she is."

He started to say something, got up instead and said, "So be it. Do you want to tell her right now?"

"No, I'm not in the mood for a scene of any kind. Why not just write her lawyers later today and inform them."

"Whatever you say."

He opened the door to find Mr. Brent waiting just outside.

"Is there anything else?" he asked.

"No," replied my lawyer. "We're finished. Thank you."

Judy was waiting by the stairs. Brent joined her, and as they started down the semicircular staircase, she glanced up for a moment, flashed a smile at me and silently mouthed, " 'By, Mel."

In that instant, I knew she knew. And I knew she knew I knew.

I waved at her and said, "So long, Sadie."

That's the last time I ever saw her.

Afterthoughts

The trouble with being a celebrity, beloved by millions, is the awful responsibility of that exalted position. Judy Garland, late in life, found herself unable to meet the demands of consistency expected of her. She fell back on the generosity of that seemingly limitless army of adoring people from every corner of the world who loved her unconditionally, forgave her for her transgressions and cheered her on. During the many occasions when she could not perform because of a "sore throat," or a cold or congenital laryngitis, one could hear cries from the audience of, "That's all right, Judy, we love you anyway. Just do the best you can. It'll still be great!"

Everything must end, and in spite of a few "comeback" tries, which were lauded by the most faithful of Judy's coterie of well-wishers, the world public finally seemed to tire of her excuses, and during the last few years of her life, she suffered the humiliation of public censure in both Australia and England, the latter having been most heartbreaking to her, since her successes there at the Palladium were only exceeded by her smash engagements at the Palace in New York.

Someone once said, "I don't owe the public anything but a good performance." I ascribe to that outlook; so did Judy. But where most performers I know are physically and mentally capable of meeting that obligation, Judy, on too many occasions, was not. Eventually, even her staunchest fans became angered at having to be kept waiting for hours, only to hear their heroine sing a few songs, sometimes incoherently, make her apologies and exit long before the performance should have terminated.

It is easy to fault the pills and the liquor, but to lay the blame solely on those two deteriorating factors would be inaccurate. I always felt Judy's main problem was environmental. Far more than her dependency on barbiturates and the like, the basic cause of what she became was the early treatment she received at the hands of the movie moguls. Their shake-your-hand-in-the-little-girl's-face-and-warn-her-to-behave-herself-and-do-as-she's-told attitude made her rebel against authority and discipline in much the same way today's generation reacts. Such deep inroads were made during those Metro years that when she was free to do whatever she wanted to do she seemed unable to cope with any kind of scheduled activities, such as the regulated hours of a television series or the on-time demands of the concert tours. Opening nights, the first day of shooting on a picture, these were single-event situations she could handle. As soon as the luster, the novelty of a project wore off, she seemed to lapse into the irregular pattern of missed performances (or at least tardy ones) and flagging interest. I believe insecurity was the root of all her troubles and contributed enormously toward the downfall of her career. As I told her during the course of our professional relationship, she really did not know how good she was, and her opinion of herself, which she held to the light on rare private occasions was, perhaps, the single biggest albatross around her talented neck.

When she died, the world mourned her; in some instances because it seemed the natural thing to do, in some quarters because she stood for something, an era in the entertainment world that perhaps died with her. Some expressed regret at her passing because it would have been unseemly not to do so. Some who vilified her in life wept crocodile tears for her now that she was dead and "harmless." Some were callous: "It was only a matter of time." and "It's a wonder she lasted this long." Many thousands were deeply saddened, and to Judy's everlasting credit and memory, these were in the majority. They turned out for her in her favorite city, New York, and said a final good-by en masse, making her last public appearance one that would be remembered.

A woman wept, blotted her cheeks with Kleenex and said, "Well, she's found that rainbow now," but she was wrong. Judy had been on intimate terms with that rainbow since she had sung about it and been catapulted over it into the golden pot that was the star system of Hollywood back when movies were movies. She had dipped into the priceless cauldron with both hands and come up dripping with doubloons of all sorts: expensive clothes, cars, homes, evenings of dancing and dining at the Grove or Ciro's or the Mocambo or the Troc, weekends as a treasured guest at the Racquet Club in Palm Springs. She had received respect from virtually all of her talented peers, and she had been married to three diversely talented men, a well-known composer, a gifted director and a famous test pilot. It hadn't been all bad, being a movie star, adored, imitated, envied by millions.

And then there was the other side of the rainbow.